HOW TO BE A MILLION POUND MUM

BY STARTING YOUR OWN BUSINESS

Hazel Cushion

with Mai Davies

D1076736

Published by Accent Press Ltd – 2013

ISBN 9781908262998

Printed and bound by TJ International Ltd, Padstow, Cornwall

To my family –

for all their love and support.

CONTENTS

LEGAL

SELLING

CONTROLLING AND GROWING

READY TO LAUNCH

AND FINALLY...

INTRODUCTION

So you want to be a great mum and, ideally, a rich one too? Welcome to Million Pound Mum. This range of books offers constructive advice on how to start a business, still be a great mum and have some fun while doing it.

This is the start of the wildest ride of your life. This is when you stop thinking and start doing, when you stop wishing for a better life and start making one happen.

I'm not going to pretend that starting your own business is easy – it's not. Nor is it something for everyone, but if you have been thinking about it for a while, if you have that dream and it just won't go away, then it probably is for you.

> *"Don't limit yourself. Many people limit themselves to what they think they can do. You can go as far as your mind lets you. What you believe, remember, you can achieve."*
>
> Mary Kay Ash, Founder, Mary Kay Cosmetics

Perhaps you have an idea for a business but you don't know how to make it happen. Or you don't have an idea, you just know you could do better for yourself than slogging your way through working for someone else every day.

Whether you have an idea or not, it doesn't matter, because you've already decided it's time to be your own boss. And that's the biggest decision. No more commuting, no more working for difficult bosses, no more feeling guilty every time you need to take a day off because your child is ill. You know the future you want, now all you need to do is take your first step on that road.

Maybe you're worried that it's a scary thing to do, or that it's beyond you. But let me reassure you: if I can do it, you can do it.

My story

I never knew I could run a business and my early years certainly didn't show much promise. As a teenager I was so profoundly depressed that I attempted suicide, then spent the next 6 months in hospital. I went from being the girl doing 12 'O' levels, to leaving school with just two, and a Maths result that was so bad it was ungraded. As you can imagine, my confidence was very low. But things looked up a little when I got a place on a silversmithing course at art college. It wasn't the obvious choice for me, but beating flats sheet of silver into shape proved to be great therapy! So there's a silver lining to every cloud, quite literally in this case.

That course led me to working in Hatton Garden, the jewellery quarter in London, and after a couple of years I landed a job selling Garrard jewellery on the QE2. What an opportunity! I travelled around the world, not once but twice, and gradually worked my way up to being Shop Manager. I realise now that I was full of ideas even then. I

2

won both first and second prize in the company's suggestions competition, and was awarded the grand total of £1,000 – a lot of money back in the 80s!

The nomadic lifestyle of working on board ship set a pattern for the next few years of my life, as I continued to be the proverbial rolling stone. I met my husband and we bounced around the world together, living in Florida,

France, Bali and Dubai. We were mostly following his job as he also worked in Duty Free. There were times when I couldn't work and I found that really frustrating. Like all entrepreneurs, I have to be busy and I have to be achieving something. So I found charity work to throw myself into, and even helped set up a charity in Dubai, Gulf for Good.

It may sound glamorous, living in different countries, and there were good times, but there were also some really hard ones. While we were living in Bali we tried to start a family. I had always wanted children, but like so many other women, struggled with infertility for several years. So in 1996 we turned to IVF and miraculously, after only one attempt, it worked. And boy did it work...

Triplets! Felicity, Richard and Julia. An instant family, three beautiful bundles that all arrived at once. But then I have never been a person who does things by halves.

We were lucky, living in Bali we had lots of help with the triplets and the climate was amazing. We had two wonderful years bringing up the children, then, just before their second birthday, the Tiger economies collapsed and my husband was made redundant. It was devastating. We went from having an easy, beautiful life to having nothing. We got on a plane without even having any keys in our pockets as we didn't own a house or a car. We had no jobs, no income, no prospects and three almost-two-year olds. We had to move in with my mother-in-law for a few months.

Thankfully, my husband soon got another job setting up a beer and wine warehouse in Calais. So it was time to pack our suitcases yet again, and we moved to France. It sounds wonderful, I know, but the weather was cold and bleak and the children were often ill. It was such a shock after living in Bali. Then I came down with glandular fever, and the exhaustion from that made me realise I needed help. My mother decided to come and stay. But she wasn't used to driving in France and drove on the wrong side of the road. She was killed in the lane right outside our house – it was just before the triplets' third birthdays.

As you can imagine, the circumstances of her death made the pain of losing her almost unbearable. We decided to leave France and my husband got a job in Dubai. I was glad to leave France but remember very clearly deciding that this tragedy mustn't affect my children's lives. I'm not religious, but if my mum was ever looking down on me, I'd want to think that she would be proud of how I've coped.

My mum had always encouraged me to write and she'd left me some money. So I used a little of it to sign up for a correspondence writing course. I got quite a few articles and stories published and it gave me a real thrill to see my work in print.

But life in Dubai also came to an abrupt end. When the Twin Towers came down in 2001, we decided that it was time for the children and me to leave the Middle East, with my husband staying on to work. So I got the suitcases out again, bundled the children onto a plane, and we came back to the UK.

We ended up in West Wales because a friend of my mum's lived there and I knew she would be a great surrogate grandma. It was quite isolated, though, so I joined a writers' group. The group's leader encouraged me to do an MA in Creative Writing at a nearby college, and as I'd already turned forty this seemed an incredible opportunity. They accepted my published work instead of a BA and I started the one-year course. It was the most fun I've ever had with my clothes on! I learnt so much and it was incredibly liberating to let my creative side flow again. As part of the course we learnt how to publish a book and I was hooked. I realised being a writer was far too lonely an occupation for me, and so the big bright world of publishing beckoned.

So you see, without any business qualifications, a very small start-up fund, three small children and no support around me, I managed to start a business. I know now that if you believe in yourself and work hard, you can achieve more than you ever dreamed was possible.

If I can do it, YOU can do it. The only question you have to ask yourself is: do I WANT to do it?

If the answer to this is yes, then keep reading. If you decide to take control of your destiny and start a business, then I will hold your hand.

Mums have the skills to be entrepreneurs. They already run a corporation: it's called a household. Organising everything from homework to housekeeping, shopping to shuttling the kids around, you spend your days running from pillar to post. You have to run your life with military precision, especially if you also have a job. There aren't many CEOs who could compete with the average mum!

> What is an entrepreneur? An entrepreneur is …
>
> *a creative multi-tasker who is determined and hard-working.*

Does this sound familiar? Does it sound like you? Well, you can take those skills and apply them to making money for yourself and your family.

There are so many things I wish I'd known when I started my company, so I have put them all in this book together with the advice and experience of other business-mums. This gives you a real edge, a real advantage, but you probably have lots of questions like these:

What qualifications do I need to start a business?

Obviously if you want to set yourself up as a vet or an accountant then you will need the appropriate qualifications, but for most businesses the only qualification you need is a degree in Life Management; that is, the common sense, multi-tasking, master-of-all-things type skills that mothers generally have. Good computer and communications skills are pretty essential but otherwise you don't need qualifications for most businesses.

Having said that, you must be prepared to learn new skills so that your business can grow. One of my favourite mottos is "make every day a school day". It might not be formal learning but you will need to develop your marketing, design and communication skills.

Don't let the lack of formal qualifications hold you back, it's YOU that matters: your ideas, your drive, your ambition. You have your own unique lifetime's experience to draw on, hard times that have made you resilient, and good times that have given you the inspiration and ideas for your business.

Am I too old to start a business?

I doubt it! I was 42 when I launched Accent Press, and I know women who have successfully started businesses in their sixties. I do think that everything you learn in life gets poured into the business in the end so sometimes it's better to have had more to add to the mix. Whatever age you are, you can start a business – remember age is just a number.

> *"Age is something that doesn't matter, unless you are a cheese."*
>
> Billie Burke, Actress

Can I really run my own business and still be a great mum?

Absolutely! Imagine your life without your usual commute to work, the frustration and pressure of your job, the constant struggle to find enough hours in the day. It feels better already doesn't it? Now imagine that each day, everything you did benefitted your own company. Imagine the satisfaction and pleasure you'd get from that. Imagine your child being ill, or you getting snowed in, and still being able to achieve everything you need to. It's much easier to be a great mum when you are feeling happy and fulfilled, and the flexibility of running your own business means you could get more time to spend with your children.

> *"How do you balance growing the business with raising a family? You just do. I had a business, a lot of orders, and a baby howling for supper. You balance it. You give your baby supper first and then get your orders in. I have worked on more holidays... but what are you going to do?*
>
> Lillian Vernon, Catalogue Merchant and Online Retailer

Where do I start?

At the beginning of course! This book is full of really practical advice and tips on starting and developing a successful, profitable business.

So if you have decided that running your own business and your life is really for you, read on...

CHAPTER ONE

START HERE!

Well, you're still reading, so I imagine you want to get started. But what's your business going to be? Perhaps you have an idea already and want to know how to implement it, or perhaps you have no clue about what kind of business you want to run, you just know you want to run one.

Be honest with yourself

One of the most important things to do is to take a good hard look at yourself. It's not just about the idea you've had. A business can only succeed if the person behind it believes in it. All entrepreneurs are different and do things differently. Assess your strengths and weaknesses.

Know your values

Some people find the idea of making money hand over fist a little tacky, whereas for others it's the stuff of dreams. Some will gladly exploit others, and for some integrity is the most important quality in a person. Whatever your values, stick to them in your business. You have to like yourself whether you are rich or poor.

Understand what you want

Take time to think about your attitude to money. You have to pay the bills and have enough to bring up your children the way you want, but just having more money may not make you happy. This book is called Million Pound Mum, but that's a mindset. Only set out to make a million, if a million is what you want. You might want a business that buys you more time with your children, rather than lots of money. Perhaps you just want more control. Work out where you want to go in life, your business should be the vehicle that gets you there.

Know your strengths

Are you organised? Do you have the organisational skills to get it off the ground? Do you have the right temperament? You will need to be strong-willed even when things are not going well, and you need determination.

Can you handle working alone, and will you enjoy it? If you are used to an office environment, you might miss it. Are you going to suffer from cabin fever or will being at home be a good environment for you?

What's your attitude to risk? There will be some risk involved, and if you are risk-averse you might want to think about how much risk you are willing to handle. You may want a small lifestyle business with little risk, or you may want to build a multinational.

Get your family onside

Many mums worry that they won't be able to balance life and work and that their family will suffer. If your family are with you then you're halfway there.

I always involved my kids so they never felt that I was shutting them out. It meant I was around for them, so if they were ill I was at home and didn't have to panic about whether I could ask the boss for a day off. My triplets are now 17 and watching me running a business has taught them so much that they wouldn't have learned if I had been away in an office all day.

They learned self-reliance, how to use failure and how not be beaten by it, how to be creative to solve a problem, they learned that it's always better to try and risk failing than not to bother, that it doesn't matter if you fail, you can try again. Most of all they learned that hard work, determination and self-belief brings rewards.

Felicity, Julia and Richard, Hazel's triplets, aged 17.

Felicity: *"It was great to have Mum working from home. We could talk to her about how her day went and not just get the highlights from her 9 to 5 at the office. Work is a big part of someone's life and having Mum at home working meant we were part of it too. So it was really inspiring"*.

Richard: *"And it meant we felt we could share in Mum's success because we were there and we watched it. And we could see if she was working too hard and we could tell her to ease up a bit! We knew she was around and that if we needed her she could talk to us."*

Julia: *"There's something motivating about seeing someone you love succeeding and being fulfilled. We felt privileged we were part of the consideration of business decisions."*

They saw all of these things every day and they grew up to be bright, charming, intelligent and successful. I know I *would* say that as I'm biased, but they are such well-rounded teenagers, and I know that running my business from home has helped shape them into the people they are.

Felicity, Hazel's daughter.

"Seeing Mum run her business taught us all to aim high, and that if you put your mind to it, you can do it. She took an idea and made it work and that showed us that we can do that too. All three of us would consider starting our own business. And we'd like to pass on the lessons we learned from watching her, to our kids one day."

So get your family onside. You may worry that they will hold you back, if the children are around. But if my experience is anything to go by, they will be your greatest asset and your greatest inspiration.

What if I fail?

So what if you do? Don't fear failure. Most successful entrepreneurs see failure as an opportunity to learn. Be prepared to fail. As my daughters say to me "Mum, what's the worst that can happen?"

> *"Just get on with it! I know people who always talk, talk, talk – just throw yourself in the deep end."*
>
> Caroline Sparks, Founder and Director of Turtle Tots

Do you know how an automatic pilot works on an aeroplane? It doesn't fly the plane straight to its destination. It makes constant small errors and gets to where it's going to by constantly correcting those small errors. That's how a business works. You make mistakes all the time, and you learn from them and put them right. Sometimes your biggest mistakes will turn out to be your biggest friends because they show you the right way to do something. Learn from everything.

Be inspired…by yourself!

> *"I want my children to see a mother that works hard and is a good role model, and doing that keeps me motivated. My daughter who is nine, told me she wanted to be a dog trainer, because if she had five dogs, and their owners all paid £10, she would have £50. Clearly having a working mother is catching or something!"*
>
> Caroline Sparks, Founder and Director of Turtle Tots

There is no such thing as a typical entrepreneur. And there is no magic potion you can drink, or magic formula you can use, that will make you an instant success. But you can prepare yourself to seize opportunities and make it happen for yourself. Your strength lies in your passion and determination. Customers buy from people who are passionate about what they are selling or doing. Investors invest in businesses that have passionate people behind them.

> "*The one thing that is critical in the entrepreneurial spirit is that it's all attitude. If you think you can, then you're half way there. If you say, 'I can't,' then you're defeated.*"
>
> Debbi Fields, Founder, Mrs. Fields Cookies

Self-doubts and how to conquer them

Self-confidence comes with experience and knowledge. Every entrepreneur has doubts, even the successful ones; they keep you honest with yourself. The trick is not to let them take over.

Ask your friends and family how they see you. It's not something we ever do, and you'll be surprised at the result. We always view ourselves in a more negative way than others view us.

Why does that friend always ask your advice when she needs to make a decision? Is it because she sees you as level-headed? Why do you always get lumbered with organising events for your children's primary school? Is it because they know you'll organise things so well? How do you always manage to get the kids what they want or need even when money is tight? Is it because you've managed the household budget successfully and you've been creative with how you are going to achieve what they need?

Ask your friends, your family and people you work with how they view you and what they think your strengths are.

I am certain you will be amazed at the response and may even wonder "Are they talking about me?!"

What if I don't have the skills?

If you don't have the skills then get them or find someone who has them. Learn. Read. Absorb. My mantra is simple.

Make every day a school day!

I will say this over and over in this book but that's because it's so important. Learn from everything you do. You are already the sum of your experiences and you already know more than you think you do. So keep learning.

And if you can't learn how to do something, find someone or something that can do it for you. No-one is good at everything. If you are worried you don't have the financial acumen, get good spreadsheet and accounting software. Success is as much about instinct as it is about maths.

I found employing consultants with publishing knowledge invaluable. I could only afford to do that one day a month, but their experience and contacts made all the difference. Talking to someone with a different viewpoint was really useful as it helped me see things from a different angle. The cost of hiring them was completely worth it, they save me from making very expensive mistakes! This was particularly relevant for cover designs and making sure our books were targeted to the right market. I was making assumptions that I knew the market, but their wider experience helped me hone my range, so it would be more professional and so much more successful.

Don't listen to the Dream-Stealers

There will be plenty of doom-mongers who will try to put you off, to warn you of the dangers and try to infect you with their fear. Listen to constructive and useful advice and make your own assessments of your business ideas and how you are going to achieve your goals. Once you have decided that running a business is right for you, then set about it rationally, armed with good information.

"Success is often achieved by those who don't know that failure is inevitable".

Coco Chanel

****

"No one makes a penny by being negative"

Karren Brady, Vice Chair, West Ham United

For more information, please visit the website:
www.millionpoundmums.com

or scan the QR code below

CHAPTER TWO

WHAT KIND OF BUSINESS?

If you haven't got your perfect business idea yet, then it's time to get creative. Give yourself permission to daydream, the best ideas pop up when you're not really trying to find an answer. Let your subconscious mind help you find a solution, you'll be amazed at what bounces back.

> *"Even if you don't have the perfect idea to begin with, you can likely adapt."*
>
> Victoria Ransom, Co-founder, Wildfire Interactive

You want to be a million-pound mum, not a million-pound loner. So use your family to help you brainstorm. After all, they'll be living closely with whatever it is you decide to do. Encourage the people close to you to think about opportunities. They know you, and they know your strengths and your passions. Let their insights guide you.

Some successful entrepreneurs ask their staff to come up with a list of ideas every Monday morning. Most of those ideas will go straight in the bin, but every now and then, one of those items on their list will turn out to be a winner. Making lists of ideas encourages you to think creatively. No idea is too stupid! Out of what seems like a crazy thought might come the answer, and one you wouldn't have found if you were just thinking in straight lines.

We brainstorm for new title ideas. We all sit around with steaming mugs of tea and talk about books that are doing well and new niches we could explore. In fact this series of book came out of one of those sessions. I laughed at the time, but then I went home and thought about it. Then I chatted to other women who all said they would find it really useful. I realised there was a gap in the market for some really direct advice from the trenches!

> *"I had to make my own living and my own opportunity! But I made it! Don't sit down and wait for the opportunities to come. Get up and make them."*
>
> Madam C.J. Walker, founder, Madam C.J. Walker Manufacturing Company, and regarded as the first self-made female millionaire in US history

Once you have hit on an idea, see who else has hit on it too. Google is your friend here, go online and search for other businesses already doing it. You will get lots of ideas from the ways other people are running this business.

A few notes of caution. Beware of thinking that because you have a hobby, you can turn it into a money-spinner. You may be right, but more often than not, people who try to turn their hobby into a commercial enterprise fail. Check to see how many people are willing to spend their hard-earned cash on your idea. Also, beware of seasonal businesses. Selling really creative Christmas decorations isn't going to keep you afloat all year round.

Start with yourself

Start with your CV. If you already have a skill base then start a business in a market place you already know, or using skills you already have.

I started my publishing business after doing an M.A. in creative writing. As part of the course we learned about how to put books together and how the publishing process worked. I loved it! The whole course was good but this was the bit that really had me fired up. And because I had already acquired the knowledge, when it came to starting up a publishing company, the learning curve wasn't as steep as it would have been had I started the business cold, with no knowledge at all.

Starting with an idea

"Whatever you do, be different – that was the advice my mother gave me, and I can't think of better advice for an entrepreneur. If you're different, you will stand out."

Anita Roddick, Founder of The Body Shop

But what if you get an idea that has absolutely nothing to do with your experience? Should you give up and look for something that matches your CV? Not necessarily. A passion for exploring a new world can be as powerful a driver as an existing passion. If you believe in the idea then it's worth looking at.

Anita Roddick had no experience of running a business before starting The Body Shop, and no experience of the retail industry.

"The reason I chose cosmetics is because of my travels, I learnt right from the grass roots as to what you should put on your body. I shouldn't have survived, there were only 20 products in a tiny shop, but it had amazing creativity, because we had no money".

Anita Roddick said the business shouldn't have survived, but it survived and thrived, being worth £700 million at its peak.

Remember: every expert started off knowing nothing. If you think you have no business acumen and no clue how to start, this simply means that you are open-minded and more likely to be creative in your thinking.

Finding the right business idea

Remember: you don't have to re-invent the wheel. You've heard the phrase "there's nothing new under the sun"? Your idea doesn't have to be ground-breaking or totally original, you can modify an existing idea. But it will need to be different in some way, it will need some unique factors to make it stand out from the rest. It will need a USP (Unique Selling Point). That USP may not necessarily be the product or service but how you market it, or how you deal with clients, or how you present it. There has to be something unique or an innovative twist that you are passionate about.

Ask some basic questions

What products or services do people need or want that you could provide them with? There's no point trying to flog something nobody wants, no matter how good it is.

If there is stiff competition in the marketplace, ask yourself how can you offer them those products or services better or cheaper or faster than everyone else?

Look for growth markets

Ring suppliers of the kinds of products or services you are thinking of dealing in. See if they'll tell you what their best sellers are. Is the market growing or contracting?

Go online. Research the popularity of an idea. You can type in a word that describes your business, something like "Organic Skin Care" and then type "discussion" or "message board". Have a look to see what people are saying. Is there a gap you could exploit? Is it a niche that you could target or is it a market that's flooded already? If there is a lot of competition is there something you could do differently? Find out what problems people want solved.

Contact professional bodies and trade associations. They may have a wealth of information on the direction of the market and which areas are growing.

Look for a gap in the market

Remember your travels. Have you seen an idea abroad you think could be adapted to the UK market? Simon

Woodroffe of Yo Sushi noticed that conveyor belt Sushi Bars were everywhere in Japan, nothing special, just like an average British café. He took the concept and took it up-market and introduced it to Britain.

You don't even have to go abroad to get inspiration. Have you ever bought a collapsible scooter for one of your children? You probably bought it from Dominic McVey. He spotted them online available from the USA when he was 13 years old. He ordered one, sold it, then ordered two more. It wasn't long before he was a teenage millionaire.

Inspiration can strike at very unlikely moments. Vision Express was born when the founder had to comfort his wife, who was crying because her optician told her she'd have to wait a week for her new glasses. Sahar Hashemi who started Coffee Republic wondered why you couldn't order a slim cinnamon latte in London when they were easy to get in New York.

You could already get Japanese food, glasses, scooters and coffee in Britain, but not in the way these entrepreneurs sold it.

For my company, it was realising that no-one was doing quality erotic fiction aimed at women and couples that made people feel good, and didn't have the 'ick' factor! There is a reason the words monogamy and monotony are so similar, and so short erotic stories can switch you from mother to lover in 5 minutes. I discovered this gap in the market from chatting to girlfriends, long before *50 Shades of Grey* took over the bookshelves in every supermarket. My friends were all moaning, and that's when the light bulb went on. I realised that if this small group of women ALL wanted this kind of fiction, then there must be an enormous gap in the market. Today **Xcite Books** is 70% of my business and an international brand. All from a girlie chat over a glass of wine.

TOP TIP

Keep a notebook in your handbag, by your bed: wherever you are, it needs to be nearby. Inspiration can strike at any time. You could see an advert on a bus, overhear a conversation in a café or see something on the TV that sets off a light bulb of inspiration.

What type of business?

Repeat business

Many savvy entrepreneurs look for products or services that will give them repeat business. If you provide something people need again and again then you'll build up a customer base and those people will keep coming back. This year I will be launching a subscription magazine on the iTunes Newsstand which will not only generate repeat income but offers a marketing platform to a whole new readership. So repeat business has more than one advantage.

Up-selling

Some products may be the type that a consumer only buys

once in a while. But that doesn't mean you won't see that customer again. Think of ways you could up-sell to them.

For instance you could sell fitness clothing and use that to up-sell fitness DVDs, sports heart-rate monitors and nutrition books. You might even expand and pay an APP designer to design a fitness app and license it.

Fans of the erotic books we publish at Xcite also benefit from links to sex toy retailers, and we collect the affiliate fee. So you don't necessarily have to up-sell your own products.

Licensing

It is possible to make a fortune licensing and selling information. If you are a life coach, consider doing workshops then selling the videos or audio-tapes of the workshops. You could move up to selling your information to companies who want to brand it with their own logo.

We license our content for audiobooks and sell translation rights internationally. This gives us 7% of our income and is simply monetising content we already have, so it's instant profit.

If you create a new process or a new technology, licensing can be extremely profitable. It's called "White Labelling". Literally, you create something and someone else puts their label on it. You create the work once, then make money on it several times. We have white-labelled dating sites for the Xcite range. The sites cater for specific erotic preferences.

What now?

Well now you're all fired up, you've found that one thing that's going to make you a million. You're ready to buckle up for the ride of your life. You can see your future opening up in front of you and you can't wait to set off down that road.

> *"I feel that luck is preparation meeting opportunity."*
>
> Oprah Winfrey

But now you've found your idea it's time to put it to the test and back up your idea with information.

Time to do some homework.

I didn't do my homework when I started and it was a huge mistake. It would have saved me so much time, heartache and money if I had. I printed 12,000 copies of my first book, when a more realistic number should have been 3,000. If I had made a couple of phone calls to bookshops and some research on sales figures I would have saved the cost of printing 9,000 I couldn't sell and a fair few trees! I'd like to say I've learned this lesson, but I still have a tendency to do things on a wing and prayer. I have realised this is a weakness, and do try to do my homework, so I strongly urge you to do yours!

If your kids are grumbling over having to do their geography coursework or yawning over their latest English essay then sit down with them and do your own homework. So you get to do your research, they can't shirk because you're sitting with them and you're all spending time together.

Don't be daunted by this prospect, the more work you do now, the easier it will be later. And you don't have to do it all in one go. An hour a day soon adds up to a great deal of knowledge and know-how. An added bonus is you'll be showing your kids how important homework is, a lesson they'll be grateful for later in life. They'll see that homework isn't just some random and dreary activity but something useful and potentially profitable. They might even have some inspirational thoughts on what you're studying. And remember: it's bound to be more fun than double geography!

TOP TIP

Find a business mentor, someone who has already made a success of their business even if it's wildly different from yours. People can often be incredibly generous with their time and experience. They've got there through hard work and they want to share that. And if they've made lots of mistakes along the way, they can steer you away from making those same mistakes. Don't worry though, you'll still make plenty of your own, and a business mentor will help you understand that that's OK.

For more information, please visit the website:
www.millionpoundmums.com

or scan the QR code below

CHAPTER THREE

DOING YOUR HOMEWORK

Now this should be fun! It's vitally important, but you should also try and enjoy the adventure of researching your new business idea. There may well be a niche you discover, or a real opportunity to make a business that will work for you.

When you are looking at the pros and cons, it's important to have a yardstick by which to measure your new idea and its potential. At the end of the day, when you take away all the whistles and bells, it's about one thing…turning a profit.

> *"I started The Body Shop in 1976 simply to create a livelihood for myself and my two daughters, while my husband, Gordon, was trekking across the Americas. I had no training or experience and my only business acumen was Gordon's advice to take sales of £300 a week. Nobody talks about entrepreneurship as survival, but that's exactly what it is and what nurtures creative thinking. Running that first shop taught me business is not financial science; it's about trading: buying and selling."*
>
> Anita Roddick, Founder, The Body Shop

So let's make a checklist of the things you need to make sure you've considered and researched.

Cost

How much money will it cost you to start this business? Is that sum of money something you already have or something you could raise? In my experience, things usually take longer and cost more than you think so don't underestimate the cost.

When budgeting your start-up costs, you don't need a fancy office but you do need decent computers. Make sure you budget for the right things.

Think about focussing on ideas that can utilise your expertise and experience rather than the ones that need huge investment.

Demand

Are there enough customers for your products or services? You may think your idea is fabulous but if there is no demand for it, and you can't create the demand you will go under pretty quickly.

This may seem like a chicken-and-egg question. Sometimes it's hard to know if there is a demand until you've produced the product. But some simple market research is essential and will let you know if you are on the right track.

We use internet survey websites like www.surveymonkey.com for this. They offer a low cost way of creating surveys that work well with social media like Facebook and Twitter. You can quickly create a survey with any questions you want, to assess whether there actually a demand for your product or service. And if there is, the responses will be your first link to potential customers.

> *"It's hard to go back and rebrand, so when you start up – start with something to define yourself in the market. Then stick with that brand in everything you do."*
>
> Nicola Sankey, Founder of Choose Nutrition

Market maturity

Make sure you face a healthy or a growing market. There's no point trying to sell something there's a dropping demand for, and be cautious of engaging in a technology that's going to be out of date soon.

I chose to enter the e-book market because it's a market with so many advantages. The profits are higher than traditional print books, and we can reach an international readership without added costs. It's a rapidly growing market.

There were extra costs for us when we started because there were so many different formats, but we went into this market early. Now the formats have been standardised, our costs are less and our profits more, and we have carved ourselves a solid niche in this new market.

Outside influences

What political, social, environmental or technological

changes could affect your business? Be aware of any developments or legislation that could affect your ability to make a profit long-term.

Does the business depend on me?

Would the business fold if you weren't in it? For instance, if you are thinking of starting a training business, do you have to be the trainer, or could you hire people once you have enough business? If the business depends on you totally, you have to think about what happens if you can't work for some reason. You also need to realise that it will be difficult to sell your business if you are an integral part of it that can't be replaced. I started a publishing company, so I know if I wish to sell my company, it's the profitable catalogue of published books that will make it attractive to buyers, not me.

As an owner it is always a good idea to position yourself to work ON your business, not IN it. It may take time to achieve this, but if you make this your goal, you'll stand a better chance of being able to step away when you need to.

Where are the customers?

It's important to know where your customers are and how you are going to get to them. Is your business one that will attract people to come back again and again? Once you have a customer, as long as you treat them well they will come back, so you don't have to spend more money attracting them. If your customers will be one-off buyers, is there a big enough demand and will you be able to access enough potential single-purchase customers? Work out how you will communicate with your customers and how much that will cost.

We use a service called www.mailchimp.com which enables you to quickly build opt-in mailing databases for communicating with and getting to understand your customers. I would suggest you start using something like this from day one.

Why will they buy from me?

There will be competition in the market. If there isn't, then it's unlikely your business is viable as no-one else has found a way to trade in that space. So, you have to know how you are going to attract customers away from the competition. Can you offer them something unique or better value for money? Define your product or service.

Compared to your competitors is your product ...

- Cheaper?

- Faster?

- Better?

- Different?

It may be that you will have to use your personality to create an edge in the early days. Later when you have built your brand and reputation, you will need to continue to inspire your team to promote the core company values.

So who is my competition?

So you've looked at your business idea and tested whether it's a goer, so what do you do now? Well you need to understand the market and what's out there already. You have to look at who is operating in this space already and how you might position your business in this market.

For my company, I realised that books were a unique product. Unlike a tin of baked beans, where if a supermarket has the leading brand and their own brand, there would be no room for a newcomer. A book if correctly packaged and promoted stands on its content alone. So in the 'cheaper, faster, better, different' equation, we ticked the 'different' box. Later as we entered the e-book market we ticked the 'cheaper' and 'faster' boxes. Quality is a core business value for us, so we strive to tick the 'better' box too.

But how do you study the competition? Paying for expensive market research may not be an option if you are just starting out, so you have to be creative.

Most companies have a website these days, even if it's just a one-page information site rather than a full-blown ecommerce site. Find your competitors on Google or look in directories where they might be listed. Note what they're offering and how they are selling it, and see if there are any gaps in their service. Are they direct competition? Is there a brochure or catalogue you can order to study what they're offering?

Talk to the competition. If they deal directly with customers, ring them as a potential customer and see how they deal with the public. Could you do it better? If they have a shop, visit the shop and see how fast the tills are ringing and what people are buying. Note how the staff deal with customers. Ask questions – do you deliver? How much will delivery cost? Work out how much floor space is dedicated to certain products.

If it's an online business and they have a phone ordering service, ring them and see how efficient they are. If you want to sell household appliances ask them which is their best-selling kettle. If they want to know why you are asking, then just tell them that the most popular kettle is obviously very good and you want to buy a good one!

There is a lot of free information out there on companies, if you know where to look. You can download free information from Companies House (www.companieshouse.gov.uk). Be careful not to draw the wrong conclusions though. A company with a deficit in their accounts may have invested heavily in a new product or service that's about to take off.

Look at the trade press for trends in the marketplace and visit trade shows or conferences to see what new products or services are about to hit the market. Introduce yourself to suppliers and other exhibitors and ask questions.

Look for published statistics. There are huge amounts of information available, from government reports to detailed market research surveys from companies like Mintel or ICC.

Use Google alerts to send you emails with links to pages relevant to your business. You can find those links by using what Google calls 'keywords', so for instance I would have used words like 'reading groups', 'book clubs', and 'crime fiction', to assess the demand and see how other publishers were marketing their books.

It's not about one piece of information; it's about building a picture. You want to find your competitors' weak spots because that's where you could find your edge in the market. By understanding your competitors you'll be able to understand what benefits your customers will look for.

If there is a huge amount of competition, don't be put off, that doesn't mean you can't find a place for your business. Just because there are big players in your area doesn't mean you can't reach customers and get yourself noticed.

I realised that I was never going to be Random House, but always aimed to make my books look as if they had come from a big publishing house, so they'd sit quite comfortably on the 3-for-2 table at Waterstones. At the time I started Accent Press, desktop publishing had just made it possible to do the jobs that traditionally would have involved a typesetter, a proof-reader and all sorts of other people I couldn't afford. So there was room in the market for a minnow like me to swim with the big fish.

> *"If you think you're too small to have an impact, try going to bed with a mosquito."*
>
> Anita Roddick, Founder, The Body Shop

The competition is much too big!

Every company has a weakness, and if your competition is a big company then that could be their vulnerability. Richard Branson of Virgin Group calls it the 'Big Bad Wolf' theory.

"We look for the big bad wolves who are dramatically overcharging and under-delivering".

You may be able to offer faster or more personalised service. So don't be afraid to be a small fish in a big pond.

And don't be paralysed by the market research. You also have to allow room for your instinct. If you believe in your idea, and your ability to start the business and carry on through thick and thin, then sometimes you just have to take a risk.

Simon Woodroffe of Yo! Sushi didn't analyse the market for his sushi bars. That may seem like madness but he's built an incredible brand. When he started, conveyor-belt sushi bars seemed like a strange idea; now they're everywhere.

"If I'd gone out and done 'gap in the market' and researched conveyor-belt sushi in those days, with robots serving the drinks, it would've come back negative, and everyone would have said 'you've got to be joking'. But I did it because I had a gut instinct it would work.'

"Trust your instincts."
Estee Lauder

Targeting your customers.

Even if you don't do in-depth research on your market, you must target your market. You can't build a marketing plan until you know who you are marketing to.

Who are they?

This is called demographics. Are your customers women over 50, are they upwardly-mobile commuters, are they stay-at-home mums, are they teenage boys? Are your customers local or are you going to run an e-commerce site that will send products worldwide? How much money do they have to spend?

How do they buy?

This is also very important. It's called psychographics and looks into the psychology of buying. Are they impulse buyers, how often do they buy, are they canny shoppers who look for value for money or are they status-driven and looking for aspirational products and services?

And remember: don't assume that if your customer has a low income that they will always be looking for cheap products. They may also be aspirational. Someone with a part-time job may want to buy a £500 cosmetic treatment because she's saved for it for over a year.

Knowing how your customers buy will help you to determine how you price your products. You can either 'pile them high and sell them cheap', or you can concentrate on high quality. Is your product the high-cost, high-quality option, or the low-cost, high-value option? You can't be both, and you can't be all things to all people. If you opt for selling at the lowest price you might not make much money per product, but you may sell in high volumes. On the other hand if you sell higher quality products or charge more, you may sell fewer but make more money per unit. Your customers may be looking for long-term durability and reliability or they may be looking for the cheapest.

Write a profile of your customers. Try to imagine what your typical customer is like, how they live their life and what makes them tick. Then work out what makes them buy and what they want. What problem do they want solved that you can solve? What do they value – saving time, luxury, value for money or feel-good products and services? Work out how they source the products they want? Do they read online reviews, do they ask friends for recommendations or do they search on price?

Once you have worked out who your target audience is, find a niche within your target. These will be your best customers. They will be an easily identifiable group with common needs, tastes and characteristics. If you can tailor your offering to this group you stand a good chance of starting your business off successfully.

Exit plan

It may feel a little strange thinking about this before you've got off the ground but you should be thinking about how you will get out. When will you sell your business? You are likely to sell it at some point, whether now or in 30 years' time. The more profitable you can make your company the more it will be worth to a buyer.

TOP TIP

Ask yourself the **Four M Questions**.

"Can I run this business and still be a good **Mum**?"

"Do I have the **Money** to start this business and pay the bills before I make a profit?"

"Can I **Manage** this business and make it work?"

"Am I **Motivated** enough to start this business and keep going?"

You have to answer **YES** to **all four** questions. If you can't it's time to think again. But if you can, then it's time to get started.

It all looks good … so what next?

Now you've decided whether or not your idea is viable, you have to decide if you can and want to do it. You can draw up the all business plans in the world, fill your files with estimates and cash-flow forecasts, you can do risk assessments on every aspect of your potential business. But, at the end of the day, it will still be a gamble. Only you can know whether you have what it takes.

For more information, please visit the website:
www.millionpoundmums.com

or scan the QR code below

CHAPTER FOUR

WHAT'S YOUR BRAND?

Now you've decided what kind of business you want to run and that you definitely want to start your business it's time to define your brand. There will be competition for your customers so how will your brand stand out from theirs? Who are you and what do you stand for? What kind of image do you want for your business? You have to stand out if you want to be successful especially if there are strong brands in your market already.

Branding isn't just about getting your customer to choose you over your competitors; it's about getting your customer to see you as the only solution to their problem. A good brand is clear and easy to identify and remember. It is well targeted and consistent.

Stick to your core values and your customer profile when you are branding. You don't want to be seen as hip and funky if you are selling period furniture. Make sure it is a brand that will resonate with the customers you are targeting.

Many customers are tired of the big brands and are looking for something original. But your message has to be clear and it has to resonate with your potential customers. Put simply, your brand is your promise to your customer.

What are the elements that make up a brand? It's a collection of things and they all have to work together to make sure your message is consistent.

Your brand is…

- Name
- Logo
- Style
- Slogan, Strapline or Mission Statement
- Advertising
- Packaging
- Publicity
- Promotion and Marketing

> *"A mediocre idea that generates enthusiasm will go farther than a great idea that inspires no one."*
>
> Mary Kay Ash, Founder, Mary Kay Cosmetics

The sum of these parts is the personality of your brand and it needs to be a personality you are proud of, are passionate about and can communicate easily to other people. Those people include your staff. They have to understand the personality of your business and buy into it, so when they talk about the business, everyone is singing from the same hymn sheet.

I thought mission statements were a bit of a joke, and a bit too corporate, but spending time coming up with one sentence that defines what you want your company to be and achieve is really useful.

It will help you enormously when you come to buy services. If you are commissioning a logo or flyers it will help the designer hugely if you can communicate this personality to him or her. If you manage to get journalists interested in something you are doing, your message and brand needs to be consistent and easy to convey.

TOP TIP

You do not need to spend a fortune on creative advertising to build a brand. Get some pen and paper and doodle until you feel you have the essence of your brand. On a site like www.fiverr.com you'll find people who will put your ideas into a usable format for just $5.

Putting your brand together

You're a mum. When the midwife put your first-born into your arms, had you already chosen a name or did you have to think about it for a few days while your little one's personality started to emerge?

When you chose the name did you agonise over making sure it was a name that …

- Sounded attractive?
- Would be easy to spell or remember?
- Would last a lifetime without going out of fashion?
- Would suit your child and his/her personality?
- Would go well with your surname?

Names are incredibly important, and your business is your baby, so you will want to consider the same things you considered when you named your child.

Is it a name that is…

- Is attractive?
- Easy to spell and remember?
- Will stand the test of time?
- Will suit the personality of the brand?
- Will match the services or products?

The right name will feel good so go with your gut feeling. You may want a name that doesn't mean anything but sounds and feels great. What does Amazon have to do with books or Subway with sandwiches? But you may want a name that 'does what it says on the tin'. EasyJet, VisionExpress and Build-a-Bear signal instantly what they are selling.

My publishing company is called Accent Press, I chose the name because I thought it sounded up-market and classy. I created the logo, an 'Á' with an accent, because I used to live in France, and it was a perfect visual interpretation of the word and the company name. I created it in Microsoft Word in 5 minutes and saved a fortune because I didn't have to pay a designer. Sometimes the simplest solution is the best one!

When I decided to publish erotic fiction, I came up with Xcite Books (www.xcitebooks.com). It's the perfect combination of 'excite' and 'X-rated'. The name tells you what the product is and what you will get from it, all in 5 letters. Again the brand logo was created in Word.

So how do you come up with a name? Brainstorming is a great way to test out names. Invite your family and friends round for a cuppa or a glass of wine and encourage them to come up with ideas. Think of words that describe your products or what you want your customers' experience to be.

When you get your 'Eureka!' moment and you find the name you love, you have to check whether the name is available, go to the Companies House website www.companieshouse.gov.uk to see if it is already taken. Check the Patent Office website to see if it has been trademarked: http://www.ipo.gov.uk/tm.htm. You can also check trademarks at Companies House.

Then check the domain name. You may have a great company name but can't get the web address. Remember if your company name is difficult to spell or has hyphens in it, it may be difficult for people to search for you online. Remember there are no gaps between the words in a website address. There are too many companies who have found out too late, that this can literally spell disaster.

Consider these…

Experts Exchange, a knowledge base where programmers can exchange views: www.expertsexchange.com

The Italian Power Generator company: www.powergenitalia.com

Looking for a therapist? Try Therapist Finder: www.therapistfinder.com

Need a pen? Why not try Pen Island: www.penisland.net

Then of course there's the website of the First Cumming Methodist Church: www.cummingfirst.com

Although the last two might have worked for my Xcite Books brand! So type out your name as a website address and check it.

Once you have your name, register it at Companies House if you wish to be a Limited Company, you don't have to do this if you want to be a sole trader.

Stick to your core values and your customer profile when you are naming your company. Make sure it is a brand that will resonate with the customers you are targeting.

What's your message?

Every business needs a USP and you need to identify what your USP is, in order to create your strapline. Once you have it you need to make it your core message. Most companies' straplines are created from their USP.

Think of Tesco's "Every Little Helps", or Virgin Media using the sprinter Usain Bolt to advertise its superfast broadband with the strapline "Keep Up!"

TOP TIP

Offer a simple and easy to understand benefit in one clear sentence.

How do I find my USP?

You will find your USP by working out what pain or problem you are solving for your customer.

Ask yourself these questions …

Can you help your customer with their life? Everyone is busy, can you save them time? Can you make their life simpler, easier, and smoother?

Will you be getting the customer what they want faster, cheaper or with better value for money?

Can you help them achieve something – make money, save money, learn something, get promotion, find a husband?

Can you help them improve their self-esteem, make them feel better about themselves or their appearance? Can you help them feel good?

When you have answered all these questions your USP should start to emerge. Your message or your strap-line should tell your potential customer instantly what it is you are going to do for them.

The strapline for my company Accent Press is …

"Feisty, Independent Publishing"

It's only three words but it describes exactly what we do to everyone we need to communicate with, from potential book readers and potential authors to affiliate partners, distributors and book reviewers.

Your strapline is the basis of your elevator pitch. This is an American term for business message. If you were trapped in a lift with Richard Branson or Theo Paphitis could you 'sell' them your business in the time it takes to travel a couple of floors?

The elevator pitch should be about 30 seconds long and your strapline is the one-sentence version. Your strapline could be the trigger that makes people buy from you. Think how time-poor we all are these days and how much competition there is for the pounds in your purse. A brand needs to grab your attention to get you to part with your money, it needs to be clear, instant and attractive, meeting a need or a want you have. It needs to be obvious!

Logo and style

Well, now you have a name and a core message, your brand has a personality. Now it needs an appearance, it needs an image.

Think about your brand's personality when choosing colours and fonts. You don't want a pink and fluffy logo to sell video games for teenage boys.

Think about what the shape conveys. Apple targeted people who saw themselves as not running with the crowd, hence the apple that fell on Isaac Newton's head. Do you want an image or do you want to make the name your logo in colours that reflect your business? If your business is aimed at pulling companies away from big brands you may want a more cottage-industry feel to the logo. On the other hand, if you are selling gadgets or new technology you need a logo that looks slick.

Once you have your logo think of a template for your company's communications. Talk to a designer about creating a brand persona that's reflected in your fonts so that everything is consistent.

Take time to get your brand right. You don't want to find you have to re-brand once you have started getting traction in the marketplace.

TOP TIP

The foundation of your brand is your logo. Your website, packaging and promotional materials, they should all integrate your logo and communicate your brand.

For more information, please visit the website:
www.millionpoundmums.com

or scan the QR code below

CHAPTER FIVE

WHAT TYPE OF COMPANY?

You now know you want to run your own business but what type of business is right for you?

There are three types in the UK

- Sole Trader

- Limited Company

- Partnership

Choosing the right structure for you depends on the nature of your business and how many of you are involved in the start-up. Let's look at them one by one.

Sole trader

Most businesses in this country are one-man-bands operating as sole traders, everything from plumbers, cleaners, and electricians, to trainers, musicians and book-keepers.

The main advantage of being a sole trader is the simplicity. You don't need to register with Companies House; you just need an accountant who will register you with HMRC (Her Majesty's Revenue and Customs). The record keeping is simple and you get to keep all the profits after tax. Your income will also be hidden from prying eyes as your profits won't be available from records at Companies House.

The downside of being a sole trader is that your liability is not limited. If your business fails then you will have to pay out of your own pocket.

There is also sometimes a perception problem with being a sole trader. People expect certain types of companies to be Limited Companies, and some companies may only deal with you if you are Limited. But you can always move into being limited once you have tested the market as a sole trader. Check the name you want to trade under as you would if you were becoming a limited company, it will save heartache later. You don't want to build up a name for yourself then find that the 'Ltd.' name is already taken. Also you don't want to run the risk of being confused with a limited company with the same or a similar name.

Limited company

There is less risk involved if you are a limited company because your liability is 'limited'. Your business is viewed as a separate entity from you. If the company is sued, the owners are liable only for the amount invested if the business fails.

Being a limited company can make it easier to borrow money and to raise finance, and you may be perceived as being a more stable entity.

The disadvantages of being a limited company are that the administrative and regulatory paperwork is heavier than for a sole trader or partnership, and the admin and accounting costs are higher. If a director fails in their duties, they can be held legally responsible for debt. And anyone can access your filed accounts and financial reports which are public.

One advantage of being a limited company is the option of creating and selling shares in your company, which can be a good way to raise funds. This is a process I used four years after starting the company, as I needed to raise money to grow the business.

Partnership

If you want to form the business with another person you do have the option of forming a partnership rather than a limited company. You both get a percentage of the return of the business.

But a disadvantage is that you are both liable for debts just like sole traders. If your partner got the business into debt, you would become liable too.

Also, making decisions can take too long because you can't agree on everything. It can be a blessing to have someone to share the burden with and someone who can brainstorm with you, but be careful who you choose to go into business with. Make sure they are competent and have the same level of commitment as you do, as well as the same vision for the direction of the company.

"The question isn't who is going to let me, it's who is going to stop me?"

Ayn Rand, Novelist

For more information, please visit the website:
www.millionpoundmums.com

or scan the QR code below

CHAPTER SIX

WORKING FROM HOME OR FINDING PREMISES?

Being able to work from home is a major attraction for mums wanting to start a business. Travelling a few feet to go to work can feel wonderful after years of sitting in traffic or fighting your way onto the 7.30 train. Those two hours a day you spent getting to work can now be spent on your future and your children's future. Not having to do the daily commute means more time with your children at either end of the business day, although it will require some serious juggling. But then what's new? If you are a mum and you have to work, you will have learned to juggle better than most circus performers.

> *"Most of us have trouble juggling. The woman who says she doesn't is someone whom I admire but have never met."*
>
> Barbara Walters, Broadcast Journalist and Author

Now you're going to run your own business you at least have control over where you will spend your days. And that's a huge benefit. It gives you control and means you don't feel so divorced from your children. It does mean that sometimes you will still be working in the evenings but at least your children can see what you are doing, you aren't working late somewhere else.

If your children are still very tiny, you might still need childcare for a certain number of hours a day, as they will almost certainly want your attention when you can't give it. But you can work around them which is something you can't do in a job. If you have orders to process, give them supper first then process the orders afterwards. I always made sure my children had a very early bedtime! It might mean growing your business more slowly than working all the hours God sends, but you have to balance your business with your family.

Of course, you can get your children involved. When I started Accent Press I had to prepare laminated cards on chains showing some of our titles to show at the Frankfurt Book Fair. I got the kids round the table assembling them. They thought it was great fun because it was like doing crafts at home with Mum and they knew that they were helping. I also got them to help me with mailshots and getting the flyers ready to post – one folded, one filled and one stuck on the stamp. We basically played post office!

There are very good financial reasons for working from home as well. The money you save on not renting an office can be spent on things to build your business, like marketing. Why put money in a business landlord's pocket when you don't have to?

You can also create the environment you want, if you like to listen to music or Radio 4 all day you can. If you want to pace up and down talking to yourself whilst you think, no-one is going to look strangely at you, apart from the cat. Those occasional domestic emergencies won't be such a drama either. If your boiler breaks down, you can be there to let the plumber in!

If you need to hold meetings with potential suppliers or customers then you can use a coffee shop or a local hotel lounge. I guarantee that in the hotel lounge you will see most of the tables taken up with people talking earnestly over a steaming laptop. You might want to find a location that fits your business image. If you are selling art supplies then you could use an art gallery café, or if you are selling fitness drinks why not use the restaurant at your gym?

James Caan, the entrepreneur from BBC's Dragon's Den, started his business in a tiny office barely big enough for a desk. He would meet clients in reception, then suggest they pop round the corner to a coffee shop as the offices were being re-decorated and the place was a mess.

Modern technology means you can run your business on the go. Emails, cloud computing, and online banking mean you never have to be far away from your office. So find yourself a good coffee shop or hotel lounge and make it your home-from-home. You will get to know the staff which will make you feel less isolated.

If you are used to having colleagues and you are going to miss the office banter, then hook up with other mumpreneurs or friends. Skype is a wonderful tool for both business conversations and just having a 'water cooler' chat. Twitter is very good for keeping you in the loop, I use it a lot (**@HazelCushion**). You don't have to feel locked away in your home.

Too small?

Many would-be mumpreneurs are worried that their business will look too small and it will be obvious there's just one lone woman behind it. Customers want to know you are professional and have back-up to deliver what you promise. Luckily there are many ways to make your business look bigger than it is. You may be a one-woman-band but you don't have to look like one!

Where you live

If your address sounds like a typical domestic street then you can adapt your address slightly to sound commercial. Give your house a name. If you live at 43 Hillcrest Road, then how about 'Argent House, 43 Hillcrest Road'? I came across one woman running an agency out of a tiny flat. Instead of living in 'Flat 12, Prospect Court', she changed it to 'Unit 12, Prospect Court'. She still got her mail and it sounded as if she was in a business park!

Answering the phone

If you are going to be out during business hours, then consider having your calls diverted to a business answering service. A basic service won't cost a huge amount and it will sound better than diverting your calls to your mobile or leaving an answer phone to pick up the calls.

Freelancers

You may need the other people or companies to deliver your goods or services. Develop a good reliable network of freelancers who can be your associates. The other advantage of using freelancers is that you buy in the right skills for just the amount of time you need them. We use a group of different freelance cover designers and know which ones will be best suited to which book.

Children in the background

If the inevitable happens and they call you just at the point one of your children is being very vocal then you can just bluff. If people know you are running your business from home then they will understand that you may need to call them back as you child needs attention. If you are uncomfortable with admitting you are working from home, then you can always tell any business callers that you are working from home today as your child isn't well.

Feel the love

When you are a small company your clients will feel closer to you than to a big company. If you make them feel valued that's worth a lot to them. What customers need to know is that they can find you when they need you. So being able to contact you is more important than being able to visit you, unless you are running a business that requires visits, like a private nursery.

Online premises

These days your website is your shopfront, so you can comfortably work from your front bedroom as I did when I started. But make sure your website projects the right image.

Will I ever need premises?

You might well find that you want or need premises. Your business may mean you have to have space outside your home. This could be office space, warehousing, a production facility or a physical shop. You may find yourself taking on staff, which means that working from home may not be viable.

Three months after starting my company, I moved out of the front bedroom and rented a small office, then I took on an assistant. As the company grew we bought an old schoolhouse so we could live in part of it and use the refectory as an open-plan office for the staff. Now the company has grown again and my children will be leaving home to go to University in a year's time so we are moving into outside offices. The key is to know what your business needs and what you can afford.

If you are taking on premises then there are things you really must consider.

Leasing

We have outgrown the schoolhouse and we can move easily because we're not tied into a lease. So if you lease premises, don't get tied into a long lease that you can't get out of if you grow quickly, or if you need to downsize. But don't go for too short a lease either, as you might get turfed out before you are ready. Getting serviced offices is another option, as they offer monthly leases. I would recommend a renewable annual lease. You have to assess how much of an upheaval moving would be for your business, and how much notice you would need.

Liabilities

Check what you are liable for. Are you expected to pay for repairs to the fittings or the building? These could give you a nasty shock if you aren't expecting them. Also check if you have to pay service charges.

Break clauses

Make sure your lease contains break clauses. These are opportunities to literally break the lease and move out if you want to.

The neighbourhood

Look around you when you're searching for premises. What's next door or across the street could severely affect your business. You don't want to try opening a yoga and meditation centre next to a noisy school playground, or a workshop where they use drills all day.

Rates

You will have to pay rates to your local authority. Rates are dependent on your location. They can be very high, especially if you are a retail business.

Restrictions

Are there any activities you will be precluded from doing? You have to check the small print. It's no good leasing a place for a dog grooming parlour if the small print says no animals.

Power supply

Check how you are paying for your utilities. You may find that landlords meter their gas and electricity and pass on the exact cost to their customers.

Parking

If customers need to come and see you, then you may need space for them to park. If customers can't get to you they can't buy from you. See if parking comes with the lease.

TOP TIP

Don't forget that if you work from home, you must make sure you have office contents insurance and public liability insurance if other people are coming in to work with you. Remember, you can offset some of your household bills against tax as it's your workplace.

For more information, please visit the website:
www.millionpoundmums.com

or scan the QR code below

CHAPTER SEVEN

THE GRAND PLAN

So you've found your business idea, you've done your homework and you've worked out what type of company you want. That was all the theory and the planning but now it's time to start committing and to start doing.

First things first, you need a plan, a business plan.

Now I can hear you rushing out to put the kettle on, feed the cat, wondering whether you should clean the kitchen windows, anything in fact to avoid this task. If this bit of the process worries you then take comfort because you are not alone. You have had the courage to decide to start a business and you don't want to have to set it out on paper and risk someone telling you it won't work. Or perhaps just the idea of having to set out a business plan worries you.

You may be asking yourself, why do I need a formal business plan? I know what I want to do and I am sure it's going to work.

It's very easy to get caught up in the excitement of starting a new business. This is the very time to pause and put all your research down on paper in a way that shows others what you intend to do. You may need this plan to convince the bank to give you an overdraft facility to cover your cash-flow problems. You may need it to raise some finance. But even if these two things don't apply to you, it is a really good way to organise your thoughts and to spot any gaps in your planning or research.

It will also help you emotionally if you are making a leap of faith from a steady paid job. If you can see clearly how your journey will take shape it will give you confidence when you become self-employed. It also helps you see this enormous undertaking in small chunks. When you break down a huge task it suddenly appears much more do-able.

Imagine you are setting off on a long journey in the car with your kids in the back. You wouldn't set out without a map or a satnav. You wouldn't set out with no idea whether you had enough money to cover the petrol costs, or a plan for what you would do if you ran out of petrol or broke down. You wouldn't set off without your phone and possibly a few drinks or snacks to keep you going. You would definitely not set out without making sure you had planned a way to keep your kids amused, or to make sure they were fed and watered and there were enough places to stop on the way!

So, why go on your new business journey with any less planning than a long car trip?

Business plans are not static documents any more than travel plans are. Plans change. You may have heard that no business plan survives first contact with customers and in some respects this is true. But think of your business plan as a starting point, not necessarily as a prediction of how your business will unfold. As you grow and learn you will alter it to accommodate new ideas and changes in circumstance. You will incorporate more of what works and drop what doesn't.

Remember that car journey you were taking with your kids? Well, you wouldn't stick to the original route if a lorry had overturned on the road you're travelling on, or if your children decide they need yet another loo stop. Plans change, but you still wouldn't start without one.

> *"Successful people understand that you don't need to make things complicated."*
>
> Anne McKevitt, Entrepreneur, TV personality and author

A business plan should help you answer five very important questions

- How will I get to where I want to be?

- How will my business work?

- What do I need to do?

- What finances will I need?

- What do I do next?

Where do you start?

Business plans needn't be scary, and you can download free templates from the internet. Many banks have their own templates, so if you are approaching a particular bank for a loan or an overdraft facility, use their template, as it will give you an idea of what questions they want answered. But remember with any template it may not all apply to you. Only use the sections that are relevant. It is better for your plan to be concise and easy to read.

If you have an accountant, ask them for help in drawing up the financial forecasts. You can also access help from Business Link, which offers free business advice funded by the government. But you must write your plan first, any accountant or business advisor must go on the information you provide because no-one will understand your idea as well as you. It's your baby and it should reflect you and your passion.

What tone does your plan need to strike?

Your plan needs to be concise and logical and it also needs to be realistic. Don't imagine that if you puff it up it will help you raise finance or impress the bank. The business plan is for you as well as the bank, so keep it real. And besides, you don't need to exaggerate to show you will be successful, because the plan should also show your emotion and passion for the project.

Show the person who will read your plan why you want to start this business and why you want to make it work.

What do I need to put in?

An executive summary

This is a brief overview of your business, a bit like your elevator pitch but in more detail. You will need to include who you are, what you plan to offer or sell, and who your customers will be.

Marketing and sales strategy

You need to show you know who will buy from you and how you are going to reach them.

The team

This is where you set out your management team and personnel. If it is just you then you need to add your CV. You can also add any advisors you have. The focus here is on skills and experience. If you are missing some important skills and experience, you can show that you have access to help in these areas from other people. They may not be employed by you, they can be your accountant, your solicitor or a mentor. They all add skills to your company.

A SWOT analysis

SWOT stands for Strengths, Weaknesses, Opportunities and Threats. It's important for you to consider this, especially the weaknesses and threats. The bank or any potential financier will want to know that you have considered them and you have a strategy to deal with them. It will also help you to prepare for them, so that you won't be thrown into a blind panic when things don't go according to plan. Running a business isn't about making sure everything runs smoothly, because it won't. It's about being flexible enough to deal with problems and continue to grow.

- Strengths – Fill in all of your strengths. The strength of your idea, your workforce, yourself. Put your assets here

- Weaknesses – Write down any areas where your business might be exposed and how you plan to cover those gaps. For example if you have no experience of importing, you could show that you have business advisors or mentors who are experienced in this and are guiding you

- Opportunities – Think about the factors that will help your business succeed. Is there a gap in the market you are filling? Is a major competitor pricing too high? Have you got access to unique products? Whatever the opportunities lay them out here

- Threats – List all the potential threats to your business. They could be a difficulty in cash flow, a rise in currency exchange rates, or changes in legislation that affect your business

The market

Show that you have done your market research and that there is a market for your product. Include any facts and figures from analysis companies like Mintel. If you are in a specialist sector which your banker doesn't know very well, you will have to enlighten him. It might be best to find a banker who does understand your market. Some banks split their business teams into sectors.

Financial forecasts

These can often be the most daunting thing. Even if you've avoided maths and numbers most of your life, this is the point where you can't avoid them any more. But don't worry, if you have never seen a spreadsheet in your life, let alone filled one in, remember they are not alchemy they are logical. You might want to go on a training course, there may be free ones available in your area.

Alternatively, there are many tutorials online that will help you get started. The good thing about Excel spreadsheets is that you can play around with the numbers to see how they affect your bottom line. You can also do different versions, one that is very cautious, one that is optimistic and one that looks at the worst case scenario. If you can survive in the worst case scenario then that should give you comfort that you can breathe out and work to grow your business.

Your financials will help you work out your profit and loss, and your cash flow. Cash flow is crucial. You don't want to find yourself with an enormous order and not enough money to buy in the goods.

TOP TIP

If you are unsure about figures and spreadsheets, find someone to check them for you. Ask them to check the numbers and the formulas for making calculations. You want to make sure they're correct as it's easy to get formulas wrong.

Figures you must include

Revenue projections – Fill in what you expect your sales or fees to be per month.

Overheads – These are the fixed costs of operating your business that are there all year round even if you sell nothing, things like premises, equipment, staff, website maintenance, bank charges.

Variable costs – These are only incurred when you produce or import things or when you buy in services, like freight forwarding services.

VAT – You may want to be VAT registered from the outset so that you can claim VAT back on any of the goods or services you need for the business. If your sales rise above a certain level you have to be VAT registered. This means that you must add VAT to your goods and services and reclaim it on your business purchases. If you consider not being VAT registered because you want to keep the price of your products low, you may be able to provide value to your customers who cannot reclaim the VAT. But be warned. If you are successful and your sales rise, then you will have to start charging VAT. Your prices would go up suddenly, which might annoy loyal customers.

Debtor days – This is the average length of time customers make you wait to get your money.

Creditor days – This shows when you have to pay your suppliers. Do you have to pay them upfront for goods or will you have an account? Will they give you 30 days to pay?

Balance sheet and profit & loss – Good accounting software will help you produce this. But basically it is your income minus your outgoings.

Cash flow is king!

You have probably heard this statement a thousand times. Until you start your own business it probably won't mean much, but once you start it will be burned into your brain. Cash flow shows how money in and money out affects your balance each month. If people are slow to pay or you get a large order once a year, will there be enough money in the account to pay your bills or will you need a loan or an overdraft facility from the bank?

This was an area I was particularly bad in the early days of my business. Now I realise that I had far too much money tied up in stock. Had I done smaller print runs, and then re-printed as required, the unit cost would have been higher, but I wouldn't have had so much money tied up in stock that wasn't shifting. This often led the company a little too close to the edge for comfort. It meant we couldn't take on new staff when we needed to and grow the company. Far more seriously for us, a major distributor went under owing us £30,000, and we didn't have the financial cushion to cope with it. I was forced to sell shares in the company to avoid going under. If the cash flow had been better we could have weathered that storm without losing equity. Never underestimate the importance of good cash flow.

Figures you need to calculate cash flow

Start-up costs – You have to spend some money just to start your business. You may need to pay for a website, pay a charge to secure a large overdraft facility, match-fund a loan, or just buy some stock and some business cards. Whatever your costs you must know them and make sure you have the funds.

Funds – If you are borrowing or getting investment, get more than your forecast says you need. There will always be slippages and late payers. This is what your overdraft facility is for.

Sales or fees – Be conservative in your estimates here because it will be harder than you think to get paying customers.

Purchases – How do you know how much stock to buy, how many components or units of what you are selling? It will take a while to find the right levels and you will find yourself overstocking or understocking at first. If you overstock you will have spent a lot of money without much coming back and you may incur warehousing costs. If you understock then you have to tell your customers that they will have to wait, and you must factor in how much time it takes to get the goods.

VAT – It is all too easy to forget to add VAT to sales and purchases, and to allow for the quarterly payments you will have to make to HMRC (Her Majesty's Customs and Excise). This is potentially a very costly mistake when you consider that the current VAT rate is 20%! This could wreck your cash flow completely so don't forget it.

TOP TIP

Purchase larger items just before the end of a VAT quarter rather than at the beginning of the next one. This will help with your cash flow.

Tax – Make sure you have built your tax and VAT payments into your forecasts. The payments can be heart-stoppingly large if you haven't planned for them. So, plan! Two things are inevitable, they say: death and taxes. You don't want a heart attack in your first quarter!

Marketing budget – It will take time to find what styles of marketing works for your business. You will almost certainly waste a lot of this money trying strategies that don't get you customers before finding methods that do. Put more than you think into the forecast, because you need to get those customers. Without them you have no business.

Staff costs – You need to allow for staff training, sickness cover, potential maternity cover, as well as National Insurance payments.

Repayments – If you borrowed money then you will have to include the loan repayments in your cash flow forecasts.

Late payments – this can be pretty scary when you realise what effect late payments have on your cash flow. Make sure your business can cope with slippage.

Getting help with the books

You can also employ a book-keeper, even if you have an accountant. It may help to keep down your accountancy costs and it will also help you to know that someone else is checking your figures.

TOP TIP

If your spreadsheets and software scare you, you are definitely not alone. Get a good software system for business like Sage or Quickbooks.

For more information, please visit the website:
www.millionpoundmums.com

or scan the QR code below

CHAPTER EIGHT

THE BANKERS!

Just saying the word 'banker' these days can often produce a rush of rude words from almost everyone.

But every small business needs a bank and a good banker

Convincing your bank you have a good idea is important. If you need to borrow money or get a sizeable overdraft facility you will need to show them that you have a viable business with your business plan. But even if you don't need their money, it's sensible to behave as if you do. It forces you to pitch your idea which is a good test to see if you have done your homework.

And you will need a good relationship with your bank, so the more they understand your business, the way you operate and understand you, the better.

What your bank likes

Despite all the bad publicity surrounding banks and bankers you will be forming a relationship with your business banker. Bankers are people are after all, or so I'm told! And because they are people they respond to other people and not just to facts and figures.

So here are some concepts to include in your business plan. They show that you mean it, that you've thought about it, and that you can and will do it.

Commitment and vision – Show your banker that you know where you are going and that you have the will and the ability to get there. You have to be excited by your business idea or you won't have the determination to keep going. Show your excitement and determination.

Security – You may be looking to borrow money and banks usually want match funding or guarantees. If you don't have the match funding then show what you are willing to put up as a guarantee. If you aren't willing to put anything up then this will show the bank that you don't really believe in your business. It should also ring warning bells for you. If you don't believe in it why are you doing it?

Persuasiveness – If you write a persuasive business plan then your bank manager will be inclined to believe you are persuasive enough to sell your products and services.

In my experience you need a plan that will make you stand out from the crowd, and expect a few incisive questions too. Practice your pitch before the meeting.

Your banker and your best friend

Much as we like to knock the banks, a small business can't operate without one. And your relationship with your banker should be an asset. You can make your life much easier if you are frank with your banker and don't withhold information. And take an interest in your banker as a person, this is going to be a relationship and it is going to go much more smoothly if you get on.

The old days of formal and fearsome bank managers,

looking down their horn-rimmed spectacles at you and sizing you up, are gone.

Remember: YOU are now in the driving seat!

Banks are competing for your business. So enjoy the moment! Do your homework, get your business plan right and then negotiate the best deal for you.

How do I know if it's the wrong bank?

Don't forget your bank is just another supplier, and you can change your bank if you aren't happy. If you you're your banker difficult to get on with, then change. If you feel they aren't interested in helping you, but in constantly pitching you expensive products like insurance that's overpriced, then change. If good quality online banking with good customer services is not available, change. And if your banker really doesn't understand your industry, then ask for a banker that understands your sector. If there isn't one available, then, you've guessed it: change.

We use two banks, one for Accent Press and one for Xcite Books, just so we don't have all our eggs in one basket.

Do I need a business bank account?

This is a logical question as we all have a personal account, and business accounts incur a charge. If you have decided to be a sole trader then you don't need a business bank account. You can put cheques made out in your name straight into your personal account. But this can make it difficult to identify the money you've made from your business, who it's come from and who you have had to pay for business services or goods. It is much easier to separate business money into a business account, even though this will incur a charge.

If you have decided to become a limited company you must open a business account. You have to show that legally you are ensuring accountability and transparency in your business dealings.

Online banking

These days most of us are familiar with e-banking and use it for our personal accounts so this shouldn't be too daunting. The invention of online banking has revolutionised business and it is a God-send for anyone starting a small business. You have instant access to banking information so you can review your cash flow, do daily audits, and make financial transactions 24 hours a day. If you don't use internet banking you will be putting your company at a disadvantage.

It should also lower your banking costs, as a bank's charging regime usually relies on how many resources they have to put into supporting your account. Online banking minimizes the effort the bank has to make.

It also helps your business to be transparent and avoid fraud, as it creates an electronic footprint for every transaction.

Overdrafts

Almost every business needs an overdraft facility. But not all overdrafts are created equal, and you must make sure you know what you are getting. Banks charge fees to arrange overdrafts, take guarantees and anything else they can think of these days. The fees can be sizeable but are sometimes negotiable.

Work out with a cash flow forecast when you will end up needing your overdraft. This will tell you how big an overdraft you need and therefore dictate the charges to set it up. Your bank should work this out with you from your business plan.

TOP TIP

Overdrafts should only be used to cope with the unexpected and to provide working capital for the everyday trading that you do. Don't dip into it unless you have to!

For more information, please visit the website:
www.millionpoundmums.com

or scan the QR code below

CHAPTER NINE

RAISING THE MONEY

An interesting fact about women starting businesses is that they are far less likely to go to the bank for money and when they do, they ask for less. Some women find it difficult to get outside funding because they are less willing to take on the risk, or they anticipate being turned down.

According to the Women's Enterprise Task Force, women succeed at or above the rates that men do when looking for finance from banks, and they're less likely to be rejected because of poor business planning.

So why do we ask for less money?

Is it because we don't believe in ourselves and therefore our businesses? It certainly isn't because banks discriminate against us, so perhaps it's time to remember that if we can run a complicated household and hold down a job, we can certainly run our own businesses.

If you have confidence in your business, be realistic about how much money it needs. If you are worried about risk then remember if you borrow too little or get too small an investment to actually run your business successfully, that could be a bigger risk. If you have too little money your cash flow may prevent you fulfilling orders on time. It could have a really negative affect on your business in the long run.

How to raise finance

There are many different ways to raise money and there is no single best route; it depends on your needs and circumstances, and your long-term objectives.

Here are some routes worth thinking about.

Your savings or redundancy payment

This is usually where people start, and it is an important step. If you invest in your business you will take it very seriously and other people will take you seriously. It shows potential investors and banks that you stand by your idea as you've put your hard-earned cash into it. It is also your money and you won't be paying any interest or giving away any of your company in return for the cash.

Grants

Now I am a big fan of grants. When I started my business, I used a Welsh Government grant to get IT equipment and to train an assistant I had hired. It was a massive help. I still use grants today, to recruit new staff as the company grows. I use a fund called Jobs Growth Wales, which means I can offer young people really valuable work experience for six months and it helps my business.

Grants can depend on all kinds of things from type of business, location, ethnicity, gender and age. Your local Business Link should be able to advise you on what's available. You may have to match fund the grant but it's still free money for something you were going to have to pay for anyway! Apply. You don't know if you'll get the grant until you try.

Friends and family

Women are far more likely to borrow from friends and family than men when starting a business. It's very common and it can work. Just make sure everyone knows the basis on which the money is being borrowed. You don't want to sour family relations because you weren't clear. If you are paying interest on the loan make sure everyone knows the terms, and you should also draw up an agreement in writing. Don't forget if you are paying interest, there are tax implications for both you and the family member or friend you are borrowing from, and they may not know that.

Credit cards

Credit cards can get you over short-term hurdles but you should keep borrowing on these down to a minimum, a couple of thousand pounds at most. The interest rates can be very painful and it would be cheaper to get a long-term loan elsewhere.

Mortgage

One route that is cheaper than credit cards and loans is of course raising money on your mortgage. Make sure your partner agrees though! And, of course, make sure you can make the increased monthly payments.

Getting investment

If you've exhausted savings and family and friends, and you are looking for investment rather than a loan, then you could consider talking to business angels, although we seem to be calling them dragons these days thanks to the BBC show *Dragon's Den*!

Everyone who invests in your business will want a return. Your friends and family may be content with just seeing you do well, but for anyone else to risk their money, they need a big carrot. If you find yourself negotiating for finance you need to consider the demands any investor will make.

Security

They will probably ask for security, this means they want to be able to get their money back should your business go belly-up or if you default on a loan.

Personal guarantee

If you borrow money from them they may ask for a personal guarantee which is a simple legal contract to make sure that you pay the loan back if your business can't. They may ask you to use your house as security, which is called a Second Charge. It's like a personal guarantee only stronger. The investor will know there is value in your house and so their money is easier to recover.

Shares

Well if you are interested in starting a business you have probably watched *Dragon's Den*. You will have seen how sticky the negotiation can get when the dragon tells the entrepreneur how much of their company they want in return for giving them their hard-earned cash. You have to learn to value your company correctly before offering a percentage. This is of course a little difficult with a start-up as there is no real value there yet. You have to sell the dragon, or angel, on your idea and show them what they will get.

Dividends and profit share

An investor will be entitled to dividends, the proportion of your profit distributed to shareholders. But an informal investor may negotiate their own profit-sharing agreement instead.

The risk for an investor will be reflected in what they demand from you and your business. The greater the risk, the more they will want. If the risk is lower then you have more wiggle-room to negotiate. If your business is a start-up then the perceived risk will be greater. If you decide to go for investment after you have been trading for a while, the better you've kept your records and accounts the stronger your negotiating position will be. And of course if you need investment to grow your company then you will probably have a good track record already.

For more information, please visit the website:
www.millionpoundmums.com

or scan the QR code below

CHAPTER TEN

CONFIDENTIALITY AND IP

So you've been dreaming about your business idea and how it is going to make you a million pound mum. Thousands of people dream of having an 'Eureka' moment and finding the perfect business idea, so you must make sure they don't use yours. Protect your idea. You don't want someone else picking it up and running with it.

If your idea is a million-pound idea and you share it with the wrong person with the wrong level of protection, you might end up very, very sorry when you see them driving past your house in a new Mercedes van with a version of your logo on it.

There are four types of Intellectual Property.

- Patents

- Copyright

- Trademarks

- Design

If you want to protect an invention, this is done through the patenting process.

If you want to protect something more intellectual or creative, your protection comes from copyright, trademark or design registration.

All the information in this chapter is a guide to intellectual property. It isn't legal advice, but it should help you begin to understand what kind of protection you might need.

So let's look at each one in turn.

Patenting

The main purpose of a patent is to stop anyone else using your invention and passing it off as their own.

Patents allow inventors to publish and defend an invention. If a patent is granted the inventor gets a monopoly on the invention for a set time period which provides him or her with the breathing space to get investment returns from their invention. The time period is usually 20 years.

There are limits to what can be patented.

Your inventions must be new and must not have been publicly advertised in any way before the patent filing date.

It must involve an 'inventive step' that wouldn't be obvious to someone with a solid working background knowledge of the subject concerned.

The invention must be applicable to industry, that is, it must have some kind of practical application in business such as a product, industrial process or activity.

In other words it must refer to something that isn't merely intellectual.

Applying for a patent

Before you begin, you have to research whether your idea is actually new, otherwise you will not be granted a patent. You may find someone has got there before you.

Once you establish that your idea is unique, then be very discreet. Keep quiet about your plans until you have filed your patent application. Make sure that anybody you talk to about the invention has signed a confidentiality agreement or NDA (Non Disclosure Agreement). If you don't do this then your invention is considered to be "published" in the eyes of the law.

The patent office will provide searches of the technical publications related to the invention and make sure that there is what's called an "inventive step".

There are also searches of any possible infringement of someone else's patent.

> *"I always recommend, if you can, to patent or protect whatever your idea is. If you can't, you have to make your best judgment. Sometimes people don't get anywhere because they sit on something, so afraid to reveal it. And yet, in the reverse, sometimes if you expose something too widely, you can risk losing it."*
>
> Lori Greiner, Inventor and Entrepreneur

Know your market

You should already have checked whether there really is a market for what you are offering. Just because you have invented a self-cleaning lawnmower, doesn't mean that anyone will want to buy it. And can your product compete with your rivals at a competitive price? You may have invented a new type of fast-drying paint, but could you compete with Dulux? Perhaps you could really revolutionise the market with your innovative new product. But patent agents and the Patent Office should be able to offer advice on this.

Define your idea

The application has to be accompanied by a specification which includes a detailed description of the invention and a definition of its scope. If the patent goes from the Preliminary Stage through to what's called the Substantive Examination, a Patent Examiner may lay down certain objections, but you will get an opportunity to amend your application.

When applying explain clearly what your invention is, how it works, how it could be manufactured in bulk and for how much. Write down what its advantages are and include a simple drawing if it is mechanical or electrical. Then take out a patent. You can either do it yourself which is very difficult or you could use a patent agent. Drawing up patent documents is a skilled job, so it is usually better to use a patent agent. To find one contact the Chartered Institute of Patent Agents.

For a simple invention an agent may charge between £600 and £1,000. Your initial application protects your invention for a year, and although protection can be extended it becomes more expensive, especially for international patents. Try to find a company to buy or license your invention in the first year to save money.

Be warned, it is a long and drawn-out process which can take up to two years or more.

Trademarks

We have become a very visual society, and that means there's much more competition with regards to brand awareness through visual representations like logos.

A trademark provides a company with a recognizable symbol with which its products can be identified. It might be a monogram or a logo or a signature or symbol. It can be registered in law so it must be distinctive and clearly different from existing registered Trademarks.

Trademarks only apply to products and not services. To register a trademark you have to check there are no conflicting trademarks that are already registered. You can do this with the Patent Office.

The registration period for a trademark is normally 10 years. A trademark puts off competitors from copying your business idea. It can also become an asset. If your trademark becomes associated with a strong brand with a loyal consumer base, you could sell it to another business.

Design registration

It is possible to register the elements of a product in terms of its shape, design, decoration, colours, texture, contours and the materials it's made of. It is basically about protecting the aesthetic aspect of your product.

In order to qualify for registration the design must be new and have some individual characteristics which are clearly distinctive from anything that currently exists in the market. The Design Registry will check the application to see whether it is compliant with the Registered Designs Act. If compliant, the certificate of registration will give a business the exclusive right to manufacture, use or even sell the product.

But be aware that this design protection only applies to UK products, it doesn't cover imports. It is very common for manufacturers in countries like China to reverse-engineer successful products cheaply into the UK.

Copyright

Copyright protects against the unlicensed use or copying of original creative works. It can't protect ideas, only the expression of the idea in a tangible piece of work.

If you create 'intellectual' works you automatically hold the copyright on them. This lasts for 70 years.

You can't claim copyright on slogans, names or titles, although these can sometimes be trademarked. Copyrighting also gives you the 'moral rights' to your idea. This means you can object to infringements of your idea.

Copyright is automatic in the UK, you don't have to apply for it. However, it is worthwhile adding the international copyright symbol to your work:

(©) followed by the year of creation and your name.

Under international conventions, this protection extends to overseas territory. It means you control how your work is exploited for money, how it is copied, published, adapted, performed or broadcast. This can be a source of income for some businesses.

But remember, if you use contractors, they hold the copyright unless you agree otherwise. The author of a work is the first owner of any copyright. Don't wait until a prospective buyer of your business is conducting due diligence, only to discover that you don't own the copyright in the works that you have commissioned. Make sure that all contractors sign an agreement in relation to the assignment of copyright to your company, ideally before they start work.

Works that can be copyrighted are…..

- Literary works (such as computer programs and novels, but not the actual names and titles)

- Original dramatic or music works

- Original artistic work (such as photographs or paintings)

- Sound recordings (such as CDs or DVDs).

It doesn't matter how your work is sold, the physical medium isn't important. This means that your work can't be reproduced and copied just because it has been put on a new or different physical medium. The creation of illegal music file sharing websites across the Internet is a good example of where copyright laws have been used to shut down businesses due to breaches of copyright, where the medium is the Internet.

The United Kingdom copyright service offers a fee-based registration and application service, where creative works can be filed and registered in case there are any legal disputes in the future.

An infringement has to be where more than a "substantial" part of the work has been reproduced without permission of its registered owner.

There is no formal legal registration of copyright, so if you think someone has infringed your copyright, you have to take legal action to claim financial damages and to stop other people exploiting your intellectual property.

You may have been told that you can seal your copyrighted work in an envelope and post it to yourself and keep the envelope unopened. It is now a rather dated practice but it may provide useful evidence of when you wrote that document.

Ideas alone do not qualify for copyright protection. Rather, copyright protects the form of expression of ideas as original literary, dramatic, musical or artistic works, sound recordings, films, broadcasts, cable programmes or the typographical arrangement of published editions.

> *"I had a history for starting something and maybe getting halfway done. Then I'd see the same thing I was doing on the bestseller list! My ideas were right, but I hadn't done them fast enough."*
>
> Lori Greiner, Inventor and Entrepreneur

Is it worth it?

If you are asking yourself the question is it worth the cost of protecting my work, then think of a Dyson. Vacuum cleaner tycoon James Dyson famously spent many thousands of pounds on patents long before any of his products came to market. But if he hadn't, the unique cyclone technology in his vacuum cleaners could have been used by his rivals.

Pitching your idea

I mentioned Non-Disclosure Agreements earlier and it's important to get one drawn up if you are pitching an idea that should be protected. Get a lawyer experienced in your industry to help write it. Some agreements spell out exact monetary penalties if the signer is found to have breached the agreement. But be careful – you don't want an agreement so full of harsh penalties that nobody will sign it!

Without this protection you'd have a very hard time winning an infringement claim. And bear in mind it's unlikely someone will copy your idea completely, it's more likely a company would alter your product or design just enough to dodge any legal issues. Going to court is expensive. In some cases a lawyer will first send a cease-and-desist letter, describing the believed offence and requesting the offender stop producing the product and possibly pay damages. If letters don't work, the next step is usually a lawsuit.

In the end the best way to protect yourself is by being extra cautious about sharing your idea. It's worth talking to other people in your industry before deciding who you can disclose your ideas to.

To find out more about each category and what type of protection you need to look at, go to the Patents Office website at www.ipo.gov.uk.

For more information, please visit the website:
www.millionpoundmums.com

or scan the QR code below

CHAPTER ELEVEN

EMPLOYING PEOPLE AND OUTSOURCING

I strongly believe that your company will only grow if you grow the people that work in it. Without good people your business will stagnate. The people in your business should be an asset; if they're not, they're a very expensive mistake.

Before you start looking for the right people you have to know what you really want them to do. When you are recruiting you need to define the job clearly, and to explain how it fits in with your business and your plans. Write a job description and find out what the going rate is for that job. You may decide to pay more to attract a good candidate. Work out the cost of hiring someone and include everything even their ongoing training. Then calculate the return on your 'investment' in them, make sure they will make your company money by being there.

Consider what employment option best suits your needs and remember that your employees are a valuable investment, so you want to make sure you get it right.

Are you looking for someone to fill a specific skill gap or just to cope with extra workload? Is this additional workload temporary, and what affect will taking on someone new have?

Options

If you hire permanent full-time or part-time staff you have certain obligations to them. Temporary staff recruited through an agency can be an excellent choice to cover a temporary need, but you still have some obligations to them. Freelancers, consultants or contractors are generally self-employed, so there are few employer obligations. If you have decided to be a sole trader rather than a limited company, employing freelancers and contractors is your best option. You can still employ people as a limited company would but you still have to tell HMRC.

You're taking a big risk by introducing a stranger into your business and mistakes can be time consuming and costly. Here's how you can mitigate some of the risks:

- Use the right legal employment and HR forms and policies

- Have an agreed job description from day one

- Set clear expectations on the level of performance required, and how that performance will be measured

- Agree a trial period of a few months to give you a chance to assess their performance

- You must be clear on what is, and what isn't, acceptable behaviour

- Have clear and written guidelines on using the company's property and resources for personal use, including phoning and emailing

- Have a written grievance procedure and disciplinary procedure

- From 2012 it has been compulsory to either have a company pension scheme for your staff or to auto enrol them into the new National Employment Savings Trust (Nest). Small companies will have until 2017 to comply with this rule.

Once you have decided what post you want filled you have to advertise the job, then interview. Interviewing can be quite daunting if you have never done it before.

TOP TIP

Ask each candidate the same questions, it is fairer on them and makes it easier for you to compare candidates. Don't sit across the desk from them, that's intimidating. You want them to relax as you're more likely to get to know who they are and what they can offer you.

Types of questions

What should you ask your potential employees? Here's a list to get you started.

- Tell me about your career to date?

- What attracts you about the job?

- What's your greatest strength and your greatest weakness?

- What's been your greatest achievement, and your biggest mistake?

- What could you bring to my company?

- Where do you see yourself in three years' time?

- What question would you like to ask me?

> *"Surround yourself with a trusted and loyal team. It makes all the difference."*
>
> Alison Pincus, Co-Founder, One Kings Lane

You may want to ask some unusual questions that your candidate might not be expecting, which might give you more of an insight into their personality. It forces them to think out of the box and it might also get them laughing.

- What would you spend your money on if you won a million pounds on the lottery tomorrow?

- If I asked your friends to describe you in three words what would they be?

- Who do you admire most and why?

- If you could have a superhero power what would it be?

Interviewing style

Do you remember when you were last interviewed for a job? Did you feel you really left them with a good idea of who you are, or were you too nervous? Was the interview to formal to let you be you? When you are interviewing listen more than you talk, smile and say 'thank you', and ask for feedback at the end of the interview. You might want to have a second person with you, who can give a second opinion, just make sure they smile too! If your business is home-based, interview in your home if that's where you will expect them to work. It's an environment that may not suit everybody, especially if your children and dogs have access to the office area!

If you do decide to take someone on then you must comply with employment legislation. It is wise to consult an employment lawyer or HR specialist to draw up a contract that meets the needs of your business. This means you can be very specific about what's important to you and your business and what their role and responsibilities in the business will be.

TOP TIP

Even if you are absolutely certain you have found the perfect person for the job, don't offer them the job straight away. Give yourself time to think about them and the other candidates. If someone is particularly charismatic it is very easy to get carried away in the moment and think 'Yes! That's the one!'

Psychometric testing

This is a surprisingly cost-effective way to find the right staff. It helps to find the right skillset and personality for the vacancy. I use psychometric testing now to assess whether someone is suitable and the only time I make a mistake is if I ignore the testing results and go for someone I like!

Job description

You must write a clear job description. If you don't, you will regret it later. It should include...

- The tasks your employee is expected to do, and any related duties and responsibilities

- The standards of job performance you expect

- The reporting relationships. Your employee needs to know who they report to, it may be you or someone else and the lines need to be clear

- If they handle finances, they need to know the spending limits and any fiscal responsibilities

- You must also lay out the standards of acceptable behaviour

This document won't just help you and your employee to understand what you expect from them, but it will be the yardstick for evaluating their performance. If it's too general or vague, or doesn't really reflect what they will actually be doing, then it's a waste of your time and effort, and will lead to confusion and an unhappy employee. And an unhappy employee will cost you money.

Outsourcing

Remember the art of good management is delegation, you can't do it all yourself. For any business owner, letting go of a process or task that you've done yourself can be emotional, as you worry no-one will care about it as much as you. But it can also be very satisfying working with someone who can offer their own expertise and skill set.

You may need other people to take some workload from you. Outsourcing can be more hassle-free than employing someone or trying to do everything yourself.

It can bring different skills to your business and it lets you focus on what you're best at. Those tasks will be done to a higher standard than you could do them yourself and get done much quicker. Your service levels will improve and you'll only pay for people when you need them. You can pull them in quickly as required, and you will have no recruitment or training costs and no HR or payroll processes or costs to cover. And if that person goes off sick, it's up to the company you have outsourced to, to find a replacement.

It's not all rosy of course, there disadvantages too. You won't be able to look over their shoulder every day and control what they're doing. You need to find a company or partners you can trust. You'll need to give a very clear brief and agree expectations up front and in writing.

If you choose the wrong supplier there's a risk to your reputation. So check how long they've been in business, how many clients they support, if they support any of your competitors, if they've got the proper data security in place, and if they've got adequate liability insurance.

What can you outsource?

These are some of the common things small businesses will pass on to someone else.

- Telephone answering

- Bookkeeping

- Payroll

- Payment collection

- HR/Personnel

- Design and print

- Communications and copywriting

- Sales

- Marketing

TOP TIP

Don't jump into a contract, and always check references. When you decide to outsource you need to ask a lot of questions. Check if they can do what you want them to do. Also find out if your personalities and ways of working are complementary. If you are the kind of person who needs daily updates, then you are not going to work well with somebody who gives you a monthly update.

For more information, please visit the website:
www.millionpoundmums.com

or scan the QR code below

CHAPTER TWELVE

MARKETING YOUR BUSINESS

You may have the best product or service in the world, but you have to let people know it's available or there'll be a howling great hole in your new business bank account.

You have to understand why people buy and what you are offering them. People don't buy things for what they are but for what they will do for them. They will part with the cash if they want it badly enough, and they will want it badly enough if the benefit outweighs the cost.

So what are those benefits? Well there are all kinds of benefits that customers look for, and you have to work out what benefits you are putting in front of them to make them buy from you and not your competitors.

Imagine you are the customer, what question would you ask yourself when considering buying something? What makes you put your hand in your pocket? You'll probably be asking yourself these questions, which means your customer will be asking themselves these questions too:

Do I need it?

If your customer really needs something then it's easier to get a sale. If they have a dripping tap it won't be difficult to sell them a washer.

Can I afford it?

The benefit you are offering could be enormous, but if the

price is too high then no sale. If the price needs to be high you may want to offer credit card payment or instalments.

Do I like the look of it?

Appearance can be very important in our design orientated culture. If you can choose from 10 identical toasters all with 10 settings and an easily removable crumb tray, you will go for the one that looks good in your kitchen. So will your product make your customer look good, either physically or in the eyes of people who know them?

Will it buy me time?

We are so time poor in today's world that anything that provides convenience is going to be a big hit. The customer might ask herself, will it do it for me faster, simpler, easier?

Is it really good?

Any savvy internet shopper now knows to look for sites that have reviews from customers before buying. We need to know the performance of what we are getting. So consider putting testimonials or a facility to add reviews to your website.

For us, reader reviews can make or break a new book. We give books away for a few days when they're first published on review sites like www.goodreads.com, it encourages people to write reviews which help our sales.

Can I understand it?

Just because you know how to use something, that doesn't mean your customer will. There's no point offering the best cappuccino maker in the world if you need a degree in advanced engineering to make a steaming frothy cuppa.

How long will it last?

Most products these days have a built-in obsolescence, that is, they are designed only to last a certain length of time to make sure that the customer has to come back for another one at some point. You may remember that washing machine your mother had that lasted 25 years, well you won't find another like that these days. So the lifespan of the product may be important to your customer. If there are two for the same price and one will last a year longer, then guess which one is going to fly off the shelf?

Is it fashionable?

We humans are pretty fickle and no-one like to get left behind, even if you don't think you're the sort of person who likes to keep up with the Joneses. Fashion can be a strong motivator. But if your business relies on this, remember to keep up with changing trends or you could find yourself with a warehouse-full of stock when the trend moves on.

Creating your marketing plan

Too many small-business owners think marketing is something you do every six months, like a dental check-up. But your business will be much better if you get into the habit of thinking about marketing as a continuous activity. If your potential customers have heard of you, you're going to find it easier to get them to buy from you.

Marketing campaigns aren't called campaigns for nothing, they need to be planned and executed. Marketing is actually a simple concept, it's about telling people what you do and making sure that you keep telling them. Whether you do it by press release, flyers, radio ads, Facebook or on the phone, you have to actively tell them, and keep telling them.

Your message needs to stand out. How bombarded are we these days with marketing messages? They are everywhere, on the net, in taxis, on the TV, newspapers and the sides of buses. You have to be memorable and give your potential customers a reason to choose you, a reason to pay up.

Think about other people's marketing messages that struck a chord with you. What was it that made you remember them or decide to buy? In previous chapters we have looked at finding a USP for your business and a strapline, well that's where you start. This is the essence of your business and the main benefit.

You have to ask yourself four key questions

- How are you going to find customers or clients?

- How will you market and sell your products and services?

- How will you build your customer base?

- How will you get repeat business?

TOP TIP

A lot of people confuse features and benefits and focus too much on the features. You must meet the customer's needs. And if that need is one feature then why are you trying to sell them something that has ten but doesn't meet their need?

Get your company noticed

I am a shameless media tart! If there is a chance to publicise my business I take it.

When my company was in its second year, we had a book of true ghost stories book coming out for Halloween called *Scary Shorts for Halloween*, so to publicise it I hired a pumpkin outfit which I wore for publicity shots outside Carew Castle in Pembrokeshire. It was featured in our local newspaper and I also sent it to book industry publications. *Publishing News* used the photo with the caption *Is there nothing this woman won't do for publicity?* The answer of course is – No! Some people might see that caption as negative, but it got us featured and raised my profile in the publishing world.

Quirky, wacky or silly stunts can work really well, but you have to feel comfortable with what you are doing. It also has to fit with your company image. My blog tagline is "HazelNuts, nuts by name, nuts by nature!" It fits my image, but it might not fit a different company. Publicity has to be appropriate.

When my kids were little I used them with my marketing, and now they find they're still helping me out.

Julia, Hazel's daughter:

"When we were small and cute Mum used us for PR. That lasted up until we were about 10!

Now I find myself doing it too. I was interviewed recently by a newspaper for a project I had done for International Women's Day. I managed to get the name of Mum's company into the interview and made sure I spelled it for them!"

Marketing strategies

So let's have a look at some marketing strategies you can use to get your products or services out there in front of people who will pay you for them.

Social media

Facebook and Twitter have provided companies with a completely free way to market their businesses. You can create a Facebook page and post regularly, encouraging people to like your site. Although don't mistake 'Likes' for customers. What you are trying to get is recognition and traction. You can of course pay for Facebook ads, which are targeted to your customers unlike say classified ads in a newspaper. If you are aiming your products at women aged between 25 and 35, then that's who Facebook will put your ads in front of. I'll go into using social media a bit more later on in this chapter as it can be very confusing and deserves a little more attention.

Advertising

The key to advertising is frequency. Regular small ads are better than one big splash. We are bombarded with advertising every day and it's easy to forget one ad unless it's extraordinary. Regular ads will put you in a customer's mind, it will make you recognisable as a brand.

Give it away

Many companies attract new customers with free stuff. Create a limited free offer on your website that your prospects can only access if they give you their email address. They will spend time looking around your site and at your range. It then means you can send them special offers or send them a regular newsletter with updates. We have weekly newsletters to let readers know which books we have for free. It's worth it to build a network of loyal customers who will give you good reviews.

E-list

Develop your electronic mailing list, and stay in touch with your customers and potential customers. It costs nothing to send out a newsletter or notice of a special offer. Once you have a list, you create the offer and press 'Send'!

We use www.mailchimp.com which collates blog posts from our website and automatically generates a weekly newsletter.

Low cost

If you don't want to give stuff away you can always do a promotion for first-time buyers. You could offer them their first product for half price or offer them some kind of 'starter pack' that's very good value for money.

Banding together

New mothers often get a 'starter pack' of the products they'll need to look after a new baby. They are more likely to buy products they have tried. So you could hook up with several suppliers to create packs for customers and you all share the cost.

Cross-selling

If your business has a natural partnership with another business then you can cross-promote. If you have a shop that sells sportswear you can cross promote with a local gym or a personal trainer. If you are running a wedding photography business you could hook up with a cake shop that makes wedding cakes.

Become an expert

If you want people to trust what you are selling you can start by getting them to trust you. Offer yourself as an expert to newspapers, magazines, TV and radio stations. Talk radio is a very good way to get your name out there as it has a constant need for experts to comment on all kinds of subjects.

I have been on BBC radio countless times, sometimes talking about my business and sometimes just reviewing the papers! But it keeps my name and my company name out there.

You can also offer to be a speaker. Industry conferences, volunteer organizations, libraries, business groups and your local Women's Institute often need speakers for meetings or networking events.

Local media

Getting in the press is always good for publicity. Customers trust what they read in the editorial more than they trust adverts. Many people think that they have to get in the national media, but local media can be more effective. To get coverage from the local media, whether it's your local paper, TV or radio station or trade journal, you need a fresh, timely story. If you aren't confident in doing this yourself you could hire a PR company. You can usually work with them on a short-term basis if your budget is small. I have done both depending on what I was trying to promote.

If you are operating on a budget you can target publications yourself by writing your own article or a press release that is written as the story. It's vital the article is ready to run and tailored to the publication you are targeting and that you have high-resolution images ready to send. If someone is featured in the piece then make sure they are happy for their image to be used.

I once asked one of our authors to write a 1,000 article about what it was like to grow up with a mother with anorexia, to publicise her book on the same subject. I then phoned *The Guardian* newspaper's women's desk and they ran it as a double-page spread the very next day.

These days I employ an in-house PR for three days a week, but use a specialist publicist when we have a high-profile book that will require specific media contacts. When hiring a publicist you are really buying their contacts list and this can be invaluable, but do check that they really do have the contacts they are claiming. Ask to see recently placed articles.

TOP TIP

If you find a story on the BBC news website that is relevant to your business, go to the comments section at the end and leave a comment. Put your name and your business name down and make sure you look like an expert. This section is used by the BBC's UGC Unit, that's User Generated Content. If they find someone they think would make a good interviewee those details are passed on to programme producers. Check the box that asks if you wouldn't mind being contacted by a journalist. If your comment is good and a programme is looking for someone to go on air and comment on the issue, you might get a phone call!

If you do manage to get publicity, then publicise your publicity. Get permission from the publisher to reprint the article. Make photocopies and mail or email them with sales letters or any other literature you use to market your product or service. The publicity clips lend credibility to the claims you make for your products or services. Have a page on your website that shows when you've been talked about in the media. Put the radio or TV clips on your website and YouTube.

Network

Networking is crucial. Network, network, network! It's something that many people are nervous of. When I started I was nervous but I knew it had to be done so I just sailed into any room with a huge smile on my face. The one best piece of advice I can give you is to always smile. Smile, smile, smile, even if your face hurts. Think about how you respond to strangers. If there are ten people in a room you have to network with, who are you going to talk to? The one who is smiling or the nine who aren't? So if you smile people will want to talk to you, and that's when you can promote your business.

Felicity, Hazel's daughter.

"Watching Mum has taught me how important networking is and how to do it. I was shy and I would watch Mum walk into a room with a smile no matter what, even though I knew she was nervous. She would talk to anyone. When I was 16, I went for an overnight experience at a new school. I was really nervous, but I thought if Mum can do it, so can I!"

When you are networking remember to be unselfish. If you give other people referrals and ideas without a thought to your own personal gain they will remember you and know they can count on your word. And if you show an interest in what they do, and not just talk about yourself, they will be flattered by your interest and remember you.

But remember: networking is more than just getting out and meeting people.

This is what the former American Secretary of State Madeleine Albright had to say about women.

"I think women are really good at making friends and not good at networking. Men are good at networking and not necessarily making friends. That's a gross generalization, but I think it holds in many ways."

Well Madeleine should know, she had to network like mad in a world dominated by men. Networking is a way to get to know people who will do business with you or introduce you to those who will, it is not about making friends. But you can use your feminine skills as a friend-maker to your advantage as long as you target people who can be helpful to your business.

> *"In any industry you get recognition because you go above and beyond what people expect, so I always strive to do that. It means when you get it back, it comes back in spades."*
>
> Nicola Sankey, Founder and of Choose Nutrition

Business cards

If you're just starting out and don't have a business card and business stationery, get some…now! Your business card and letterhead tell prospective customers you are a professional who takes your business very seriously. It also means they carry your information away with them. But make sure they're stand-out cards. People collect business cards every day, make sure yours gets noticed.

Affiliates

One good way of harnessing the power of other people is getting affiliates. Instead of, or as well as, selling your products yourself, look for affiliates and resellers, or people who will generate leads for you. You'll have to give them a commission on sales, but as long as you make sure your pricing structure can accommodate it, then you could end up with a small army of people selling your products. We have an affiliate scheme with www.clixsgalore.com which offers commission to anyone who can drive paying customers to our sites.

Run a competition

If you run a competition, the cost of the goods you give away will probably be quite low in comparison with the amount the customer would have to pay for it, so the perceived value to them is much higher. Many magazines do product giveaways, for example some beauty magazines will run a competition where the prize has to be worth £500 to the customer, but that may only cost the small business giving the stuff away £100. To enter the competition, the customers have to enter a code on the company website. That means that all their email addresses are now in your email list and they've probably had a good look round your site.

Demonstrate

If your product or service is something that can be demonstrated, then get out to see groups that might want to buy from you, and show them how it works.

Throw a party

If it suits your product, you can find people who are willing to run a party in their house in return for some free product, then as long as they get the right sort of people in the room, this could be well worth it. Lots of companies have formal party-plan operations, like Avon and Ann Summers, but you could do some informal parties to start spreading the word. All of your friends have friends you don't know.

Pay-Per-Click advertising.

You could try out Pay Per Click (PPC) advertising on Google. They often advertise special offers that give you £50 or £75 in free advertising to start. Read the directions for the service you plan to use, and watch very carefully what you spend on a daily basis until you are comfortable using PPC ads. You can set an upper limit so that you don't go over budget. Monitor which keywords get you business and which ones are a waste of time.

A bit more about social media marketing

I want to come back to social media because it is a very effective tool but only if you use it properly. Many people think that because it's free and everyone uses it, that it will be simple to throw your products on there and the money will pour in.

The social web does make it more cost-effective than ever to get the word out about your products and services, no matter what industry you're in. Most social media accounts are free to set up, and many targeted online ad platforms are inexpensive. What it will cost you to get your campaign rolling is time and effort. That time will be spent researching how to do it and getting it right.

The toughest thing for any new business is finding a strategy to get your message heard over everyone else's message. The internet is a very noisy place.

So how do you do it?

Become an expert

I've suggested you become an expert in the real world, well you can become an expert in the virtual world too. Research active forums and online bulletin boards that are relevant to your business and audience. Join some of them and start posting expert advice to solve problems or answer questions. You will have to do this for a while before you see results but you will find that people start to become paying customers.

Advertising is not always the best way to market on social networks. What people want is valuable content, and it can be as niche as the products you're selling. By blogging, tweeting, sharing, and updating about things relevant to your industry, you can build credibility in your field.

You can write how-to articles, or create video demonstrations. You could post pictures and tweet a commentary from an industry trade show. Every piece of content you post online – whether it's on your blog, your Facebook page, or on third-party sites – has the potential to boost your brand and drive search results and traffic at very little or no cost.

YouTube can be a great place to create low-cost, high-impact content. A small investment in a video camera, some simple editing software, and a bit of time learning the basics of video production, can pay out in the long term. Put your production out on video-sharing sites, and you never know, if they're funny or really useful they might go viral!

Cultivate 'super users'

The social web has changed both the medium and the message for marketers. It's not just you who will be in control of your brand now but users. They can 'like' on Facebook, recommend, and retweet. This can be a very positive thing if you understand social media and use it to your advantage.

The key is targeting and cultivating super users, those are customers who are already fans of your brand, and share their positivity about it on the web.

For instance, if you sell handbags, do a Twitter search for a user who loves them and talks about them. You can reach out to her and offer her 20% off, to come in to your shop or check out your website. You might want to send her a new model with a note saying 'Thanks for telling people about handbags, we love you!' It's a fairly safe bet that she'll start talking about you and it'll cost you very little.

When an endorsement comes from someone outside of your company, like a trusted blogger or social sharer, it has enormous value and a much wider reach than you could achieve alone. You can't control what the social web says about your brand directly, but by identifying and courting a few brand ambassadors, you can certainly have an influence. And it's the kind of influence that no paid advertising will ever get you.

Make sure people can find you on the web

This may seem obvious, but it's a common mistake new businesses make. You can set up a free listing for your business in search engine local directories. Try google.com/local, bing.com/local and listings. local.yahoo.com. Take the time to make sure that your entry is accurate, and there are direct links to your website and phone number. And make sure there's a description of your business on there too. In fact add as many details to the list as you can, like a map and your business hours.

If the sites offer reviews, encourage your customers to post reviews of your products or services with an incentive. You could give them a 10% discount if they leave a review on the site. This encourages repeat business as well as reviews.

For more information, please visit the website:
www.millionpoundmums.com

or scan the QR code below

CHAPTER THIRTEEN

SELLING AND PRICING

Well now let's suppose you've set up your business. You've got your gorgeous business cards, your shop or your home office, you have a business bank, you've raised the money, and you are all ready to go. Now it gets real. Now you have to get people to actually pay for your products or services. There is a massive thrill in getting your first order, even if it's just for a tenner. It's your first sale and it feels wonderful.

To be successful you have to do two things, make sure you have a profitable business model and then get sales. One without the other just won't work!

> *"Nobody talks about entrepreneurship as a survival, but that's exactly what it is and what nurtures creative thinking. Running that first shop taught me business is not financial science, it's about trading, buying and selling."*
>
> Anita Roddick, Founder, The Body Shop

Pricing

We've talked about customer service, now let's look at pricing. Your price point is crucial. But how on earth do you judge what your starting price should be? This is a major decision for any business. Of course, you have to cover all your costs, but finding the right price point is always down to trial and error and as always, a little luck.

Pricing is not an exact science, it never has been and never will be. Life would be so much easier if it was! That's why companies, big ones and little ones, can spend months trying to work out where to pitch their prices. 'What should I charge?' is a question every business owner has to ask, and unfortunately it's one of the most difficult to answer.

That's because pricing, perhaps more than anything else, has the power to determine whether you sell a million or none at all.

So where do you start? Here are some ways to get it right:

Analyse the competition

While your costs will inevitably drive your pricing, don't forget the competition. In markets where there are lots of competitors, it's a very good way to work out where to start. If your products are sold in shops, go and look at the price ranges and try to work out where on the shelves your products could go. For me it was fairly easy as there seemed to be a universal price for a paperback of £6.99, which has now crept up to £7.99. Where it is harder, but often more profitable, is the pricing of hardbacks such as cookbooks. Since the demise of the Net Book Agreement, publishers have tended to price up, knowing the books will be discounted. Jamie's and Nigella's cookbooks at Christmas are usually priced at £30 but most people will buy them for half of that.

Talk to potential customers

If you haven't already launched, talking to potential customers about your prices is a really good way to get an idea. You've probably asked people if they think your business idea is a good one, now go back and ask them how much they would pay. Make sure though you ask the right people, people who would normally purchase your type of product or service. You don't want to ask your garage mechanic how much he would pay for your new range of lip gloss, not unless he regularly buys it for his wife!

Start higher, but not too high

It's almost always easier to lower your prices than to put them up. So it's generally better to overshoot than to undershoot. But don't go too high. If you price your product or service way too high, it may be difficult to get potential customers to take a second look. Customers are also cautious of permanent sales or discounts – I do sometimes wonder if anyone actually pays full price for a sofa with a certain UK firm, as one sale always seems to lead straight on to the next one!

Use discounts

Discounts can be a great way to get a 'feel' for what's right. You're not committing to a permanent price, and you can judge the response. If they fly out of the door and you are still making a healthy profit you may have found your sweet spot. Make sure you aren't under-pricing though!

Play with the packaging

Pricing doesn't exist in a vacuum. Customers don't judge a product or service on the price alone. One of the most important things people consider when they buy is perceived value. Value is very different to cost. Cost is how much you pay for something, whereas value is more subjective, it is what the customer FEELS the product is worth to them. Your job is to discover the value of your product to your customer. If you package a product or service better you could see a big rise in sales.

Listen to your customers

Customers don't usually hold back when it comes to telling you their opinion about your prices. They'll let you know pretty quickly, whether it's *"I can't believe this is only £10.99"* or *"Fifty quid? You must be joking!"*

At the end of the day, getting pricing right is a bit of an art as well as a science. It takes a combination of research, experimentation, and a big dollop of hedging thrown in.

There are many strategies for pricing and the right one for you and your products or services will depend on what you are trying to sell and the psychology of your target customers. Here are some strategies you might want to consider:

Competitive pricing

Consumers have a lot of choice and will usually shop around for the best price. I know I do! If you are considering pricing at the same level as your competition you will need to provide something to stand out against the competition. Branding may give you the edge here – do your customers trust your brand more than the competitors? What have you done to convince them that they should?

TOP TIP

It is difficult to say which component of pricing is the most important. Just remember, the right product price is the one your customer is willing to pay, that provides you with a profit.

Pricing below the competition

This simply means being cheaper. This strategy works well if you can negotiate the best prices from your suppliers, reduce costs and develop a marketing strategy to focus on special prices and discounts. This is risky though, as it is hard to then start raising your prices, and your product or services may be seen to be inferior.

Prestige pricing

This is pricing higher than your competition. You can consider this when you have something that can justify it, like location, exclusivity or unique customer service. If you stock high-quality goods that your customer can't get anywhere else, this may work well for you. But be prepared for someone else coming in on your patch. You may have to lower your prices, so make sure your margins could take it.

Psychological pricing

The most common method is odd-pricing, which is using prices that end in things like 99. Customers tend to round down a price. We've all seen it. That new kettle is £15.99. So in your head it's £15, even though it's only a penny off £16. We all know it's a trick, but it still works! If you don't believe me, just look at how you view the prices next time you are in the supermarket. Since we know this works it is always worth pricing at .99 rather than .95 – you may as well make an extra 4p on every sale!

Multiple pricing

This is where you sell more than one product for one price, like three items for £10. This is good for sales and customers very often buy more. We do this a lot with e-book bundles and it is a great way of getting customers to try a new product or, in our case, author.

Loss leaders

This is where you sell an item for less than your cost. The theory is that once customers are through your door they'll buy other products at higher margins. Think of the item as a giant carrot to get them in.

Selling

So now you have your prices right it's time to sell. The easier you make it for people to buy from you, the more you will sell. But there are many ways to sell and you may find that only one or two suit your business and you may find you need a combination. A lot will depend on the scale of your business. But you have to identify your route to market. Having a great service or a revolutionary product is useless if you don't really know how you are going to get it in front of your customers, and how to get it to them while still make a profit.

There's a variety of routes, let's have a look at them.

Retailing

You're retailing if you sell directly to your customer. You may have your own shop or online store.

Wholesaling

You can wholesale your products to other people who are retailing, but your profit margin will be lower on each unit. They need to add their mark-up to the price they buy from you. But you don't have the overheads of a shop and you probably need fewer customers as they are making larger orders. You could do a combination of wholesaling and retail.

Selling through an agent

You may want to concentrate your efforts on something other than finding people to wholesale to. If you hire a sales agent you will make less money on each unit you sell but you may get your products into more outlets. So you have to weigh up the cost against the potential profit.

We use agents to sell our translation rights as it is such a specialist skill, and they have all the contacts. It is well worth paying them a commission to do this, as they generate revenue that would almost certainly not be made without them.

Selling online

You have much lower overheads than retailing through a shop but you have to drive traffic to your website as you can't rely on footfall, that is, people wandering past and seeing your shop. You're selling at your retail price and you add postage and packing costs.

Online marketplaces such as Ebay and Amazon's Marketplace can offer great opportunities – we have sold excess books in this way, it clears stock and, by adding in a catalogue with every order, also acts as a marketing opportunity.

Recommendation

If you have an existing customer you can offer them a discount if they introduce a friend who buys something. It means you lose money on one product but you get a new customer who could introduce another and another. And if those customers become repeat customers, then your customer base will grow quite quickly.

Events and networking

Taking stock with you to events like networking lunches means you get to sell directly to new customers with no overheads. What you're aiming to achieve here is a few sales and word of mouth. If you can impress ten people in that room, each one of those people has at least ten friends. There's an adage in the book trade that for every book you sell, you will sell three more because the reader generates word-of-mouth interest.

Multi-level marketing

MLM, as it's known, involves recruiting people to sell on your behalf. You offer them commission if they get their friends to sell your stuff too. Everyone in the chain is working for commission, so to be successful you need really good systems. This is a very complicated operation to set up and you shouldn't really go into it unless you have significant financial backing and a team with experience of multi-level marketing. Lots of MLM companies spring up and go out of business just as quickly because they don't have a big enough investment or infrastructure.

Distributors and affiliates

Affiliate marketing works particularly well for online businesses. Quite simply, other people can sell your products and get a cut for doing so. You get less money per product but you have more people selling. This is especially worthwhile if you run an internet site, as you can use affiliate schemes to monetize the site and cover the website's running cost. Some sites, such as voucher or review sites, only use affiliate schemes. It's a great business model as there is no stock investment.

Direct selling and using distributors

It is often tempting to try and avoid sharing your profits with an affiliate or a distributor. Some distributors want a really high margin, up to 50%. But there are pros and cons

135

to both types of selling and you could decide on a combination of the two.

Using a distributor

Consider the fact that they may have a huge network already in place and a relationship with the audience you want to reach, so they can sell much bigger volumes than you could. They have instant access to an already 'warm' market, that is, people who are receptive to buying what you're selling.

Distributors may also know your market inside out because they sell a lot of your rivals' products. They may be able to help you price your products. They will tell you if you're overpriced, or they may just say they can't stock you because of your prices.

If you have no warehousing then distribution may be ideal for you as it saves you the cost. They often have warehousing of their own.

You may also cut some of your risk and cost. The distributor has to collect payment from the customers which reduces your risk of bad debt, and they may have cheaper delivery systems because they deliver more goods.

Sales teams could give you valuable feedback by discussing your products with potential customers. This is very useful if you are thinking of launching something new.

You must manage your distributors though if you decide to go down this route. You don't want them holding you to ransom because you've put all your eggs into the distributor basket.

How to handle distributors

- Agree targets with them so both of you focus on those targets

- Make sure they know your products so that they really sell them

- Give them incentives to hit targets, and review your targets regularly

Selling directly to the customer

If you want to keep all of your profits then you have to sell direct. But it may also make sense for you because you don't operate in a market where distributors will work for you.

There are many benefits to direct selling.

Instant feedback

If you talk to your customers then you will know pretty quickly if they are happy or not. If you sell through distribution, feedback may be patchy.

Personal

If you are providing a one-to-one service like life coaching then obviously you can only do this directly. But don't forget you may want to create an information product later on, like an e-book or an online course, which you could then sell through affiliates. But to begin with, it's a personal approach.

Word of mouth

If your business works on referrals or word of mouth, these are easier to get if you sell directly.

Service levels

You can directly control how you interact with your customers. Train your staff in high levels of customer service. You can also get loyalty from your staff who will work hard for you. You'll never get that level of loyalty from a distributor, unless there's a financial incentive for them, and financial incentives cost you and your business.

Haggling

You can negotiate a price with a customer there and then. A distributor has less wiggle room than you do, to do that.

Upselling

If you are talking to your customer you can use the opportunity to sell them additional items. This increases your profit for that single sale.

Passion

No-one is going to have your passion for what you're selling. And passion is very attractive, very often more attractive than slick sales patter.

How to sell

Now this may be the bit that worries you. But take comfort because you're not alone. It's a subject that has many budding entrepreneurs quaking with fear. You have come all this way, honed your concept, set up your bank account, bought your stock, printed your leaflets... but now you actually have to SELL!

It really isn't as scary as you think. At the end of the day it is just talking to people. As I've just said people don't like sales patter, they like talking to people.

So here are some tips.

Listen

Some business people are so focused on pushing their products on customers they don't stop to listen or look at the body language. You have to create some rapport so show some interest in your customer.

Questions

Ask open questions, questions that you can't answer with a 'yes' or a 'no'. If you are trying to sell them a washing machine, ask them things like 'How many wash cycles do you use a week?' and 'Which washing programmes do you find you use most?' Then they will then tell you exactly what they want, so you won't waste their time showing them a model with lots of features they don't need. Do you remember when I spoke earlier about 'benefits' versus 'features'? Well, find out what benefits they're looking for, then show them the product that matches it.

Closing the sale

When you establish that they want it, you have to close the sale. This is often the bit people hate doing. But they want your product, they've seen the value and the benefit, so ask for an order. Now you asked closed questions. It's at this point you'll find out any objections they have and you can answer them. And once they've ordered, remember that customer service is crucial. Get them their order on time and in the right condition without any hassle. Good customer service increases the chances they'll come back for the tumble dryer.

Don't rubbish the competition

If they're using a rival product, don't criticise it. They chose it, so you're criticising their judgement. Instead focus on why yours is better value and more beneficial to them.

Know your stuff

You have to be prepared to answer questions so make sure you know your product inside out and make sure you know your costs. You don't want to negotiate a price then get back to base and find you've sold it too cheaply.

Talk to the right person

Just because you are talking to someone and they're making lots of positive noises doesn't mean you are going to get a sale. That person may not be the one who holds the purse strings or makes the decisions.

I learnt a lot about sales when I worked in recruitment during the 1980s. The UK was in the grip of a major recession, and there were huge numbers of highly skilled people unemployed. With so many to choose from, and with companies cutting back their costs, this was a really tough time to be asking companies to pay hefty fees to recruit new staff. By pushing the benefits, though, we could make them see that instead of sifting through hundreds of CVs and conducting rounds of interviews, we could present them with five carefully selected, highly suitable candidates, and that freed them up to concentrate on running their businesses. Which, with the times being so tough and competition so fierce, was exactly what they needed to be doing.

For more information, please visit the website:
www.millionpoundmums.com

or scan the QR code below

CHAPTER FOURTEEN

BEING PROFITABLE

Well, it sounds obvious but you have to make sure you are actually making a profit. If you want your business to flourish your prices have to cover your costs. It's so easy to get lost in the figures, miss a hidden cost or forget to allow for a rising cost, and before you know it, your profit is wiped out. So you have to keep a close eye on your trading margin.

Your trading margin quite simply is the difference between your selling price and the cost of providing the service or product, minus your overheard costs. It is harder than you think to calculate your trading margins.

TOP TIP

You have to know your numbers. I know this sounds trivial, but you must get into this good habit now.

Here are a few ways to try and make sure your trading margins are accurate.

Understand the true costs of your product

This is not the price you pay for it, it's the total of ALL the costs involved, from the moment you pay for it until it gets to your customer. It includes all the costs of storing the goods and delivering them to the end customer. You see, every step in a process adds a cost. Even if you sell information products on the internet you must be careful. With information products, once you have created them, you think the rest is pure profit. But you have to make an allowance for the average amount of support time each person will need and the costs associated with that. You have to factor in the payment processor costs and any update or email marketing costs.

Buy at a good price

The less you pay the more you make. If you use a regular supplier negotiate a good deal for staying loyal. If you can buy in bulk you will usually find that the price goes down, but this only gets easier as you get more successful and are able to send in bigger orders. Don't be tempted to buy too much stock, though, just because you have been offered a good deal. If it then sits in your warehouse tying up your cash flow you will soon be in trouble – one of the main reasons companies fail is because they run out of capital to run the business, as it is all tied up in stock and assets.

Rising costs

You have to keep an eye on rising costs and you may have to increase your own prices to reflect that. It is easy to forget to update pricing if there is a postal rise, or if your credit card facility alters their pricing, but it only takes a small change to swallow all your profit if you are working on tight profit margins.

Materials

Record everything you use, it's amazing how forgetting little things can soon add up. Even paperclips and toilet rolls add up over the course of a year! The old adage 'if you look after the pennies the pounds will look after themselves' is worth remembering. I know from experience how you can get so wrapped up in working and seeing turnover rise that you lose sight of costs and therefore, profit.

Purchase orders

If you have a purchase order, your book-keeper can match this with the supplier's invoice to make sure you don't over pay. The supplier's invoice could be wrong.

Bad debts

If you suffer from clients who don't pay you have to build a figure into your pricing so you are covered for that loss.

Keep timesheets for yourself

Now this may sound a little over-the-top but you need to know how much time you are spending on any particular job. You may find you are spending too much effort on the things that don't actually make you money. You can become what's known as a 'busy fool', working IN your business instead of ON your business.

Make sure you are paid for your time

If you have to travel to see clients, make sure you build in a fee for the time it takes you to get to them and the hours you spend with them.

```
┌─────────────────────────────────────────────┐
│                   TOP TIP                     │
│                                               │
│  Keep your overheads low and focus on profit. And don't │
│  get excited about turnover. Remember the old adage:    │
│                                               │
│      Turnover is Vanity, Profit is Sanity!    │
│                                               │
└─────────────────────────────────────────────┘
```

Danger zones

There are danger zones to avoid when it comes to profit, small things that can quickly erode the profit you have worked so hard to create. The euphoria of seeing those sales come in can make you feel very secure and it is easy to slide into focussing on the day to day running of things without focussing on your profitability. Watch out for things which can quickly wipe out your hard-earned gains.

Family panic

Things go wrong in a business, always, it's a given. But that's OK, you've accepted that you know it's going to happen. But you find that your family is more panicky about it than you. Fielding problems in the business whilst fending off an avalanche of questions from your partner isn't easy. Best to work out right at the outset how you are going to handle these situations.

Over-promising and under-delivering

It is always best in business to under-promise and over-deliver. So many businesses fail because they get this the wrong way round. Do it right and you pleasantly surprise the customer who will then probably become a repeat customer. But if you over-promise and they don't get what they want, you may have to refund their money, or keep the money but never see them again. Or you may have to pay out more to get them their order quickly because you left it to that last minute, and that erodes your profit.

Last minute

I know what it's like, you are rushing around trying to get everything done and it's easy to leave some important things till the last minute. But if that's paperwork, or invoicing then your cash flow will suffer and you may end up paying for a bigger overdraft to cover it. Or you forget to include all the costs because you are rushing. If you are so busy you haven't had time to plan your purchases then you may end up paying over the odds which will hit your margins.

Late payers and bad debts

Some customers will become nightmares and won't pay you on time. Some may default altogether. If you can, set up a system where they pay in advance or pay half up front.

Being overtired

It is very easy to get exhausted trying to be a mum and run a business. When you are overtired, everything takes longer. Try to build in time to rest. It may feel like you are taking time away from the business, but if you are rested you are more productive. You get more done in an hour if you are alert than you do in six hours if you are shattered.

New staff

If your company is doing well you may take on staff. But they take time to train, which means your costs stay the same but your output falls, and so your profits will go down. This is only a short-term problem but many companies find themselves in this Catch-22 situation. The upside is that new staff can inject energy, enthusiasm and new ideas into your business and relieve you from routine jobs.

Creaking systems

You may have started your business with a simple book-keeping system, or a card-index system, but as your business grows you need more sophisticated systems or software. Upgrading takes time, and time eats into you profit. Over the last two years we have installed a title management system that now also handles our royalties. Without a doubt it was painful and, at times, frustrating, but the benefits have been massive. We now have all the information on our titles in one place, our authors love the new clearer royalty statements, and we also have an accurate profit and loss available by title. It has given the business a central core from which we can grow and expand.

Keeping customers happy

Customer service is crucial. Think about how you decide to buy things. If there's a choice between two shops, one with good service and one with not so good, it's obvious which one you will choose.

How many times have you wanted to scream down the phone when you hear an automated voice telling you that the company 'values your custom'. Oh, really? Well why are they keeping you hanging on for 15 minutes before speaking to you then?

Communication with your customer is crucial. They need to feel they know what's going on. One easy way to keep in touch with your customers is by automating that communication. Look at Amazon. When you place an order you instantly get an email that thanks you for your order with an estimated despatch date. Then you get another email to say it's been despatched. It's an automated system that keeps the customer happy.

It's an old cliché that the customer is king but it's true. Without customers you have nothing. You don't just want to sell to them, you want to keep them, because getting repeat business is easier and cheaper than getting new customers.

And word of mouth is better than any advertising. If your customers are happy they'll recommend you, either in person or on online review sites, or in the review section of your own site. You want 5 stars from every customer!

I have a friend who recently bought a pair of handmade tango shoes over the internet from a shop in Argentina. She was taking a bit of a risk as they were made-to-measure and she had to draw around her foot on a piece of paper and send in various measurements. But they were £70 which was half the price of buying them in a shop in the UK. Her shoes arrived on time but the shoebox had been squashed on its travels from Buenos Aires. The shoes were wonderful but she was miffed about the box and thought the company should provide better packaging.

But before she could complain, an email landed in her inbox, sent personally by the manager, asking if she had tried on her shoes or danced in them and asking if they were comfortable. She was so pleasantly surprised she wrote back to say that indeed she had and they were very comfortable. A few friendly emails pinged back and forth and she quite forgot about the box. And guess what? She has recommended the shop to all her tango dance class who have gone to that website to buy shoes at such a good price because they know they can trust the service. So, a few personal emails netted that shop quite a few extra customers, who will probably be customers for life.

The rule is pretty simple, treat customers the way you would like to be treated. Imagine you're the person at the other end. What would be their experience of buying goods and services from you?

So how do you know if your customers are happy? If they buy from you face to face you can tell pretty quickly and you can ask them. But what if they don't?

Get feedback from them. Create a customer checklist, something that isn't difficult or time-consuming. Ask them to rate your service. If something has a low score, work to improve it. Offer them plenty of ways to complain, you don't want to avoid complaints, you want to hear them so you can put things right. If you turn an unhappy customer into a happy one they may well become a repeat customer because they feel taken care of. And if they come back, they will bring their friends.

Create a customer service policy

Make sure all your staff are singing off the same hymn sheet. They should all handle complaints the same way. Your company is only as good as the people in it. If a customer rings up furious and speaks to the one weak link in your company who handles him or her badly then that customer is gone. Your staff need clear processes to follow, so make sure your targets can be measured, for instance calls should be answered within 5 rings, calls should be returned within two hours, emails should be replied to within 24 hours.

You can test this out by asking someone you know to step into your customers' shoes for a day. Ask them to test the system by ringing in or trying to order something and then complaining. See how it's handled. How do the products arrive? Is the packaging good enough? Does the delivery service you use deliver when they say they will or are they late?

Keeping your customers

As I've said before, it's easier to get repeat customers than to get new ones. It's also easy to forget your customer once they have bought from you. It might well be worth investing in Customer Relationship Management software, or CRM as it's known.

It will help you record contacts and stay on top of managing them. Once you have customers, you can upsell additional products and services to them. You can offer them a discount if they introduce a friend. If you sell them a product that lasts 3 months, you can contact them just before they are due to run out and offer them another.

"The customer's perception is your reality."

Kate Zabriskie, Author of *Customer Service Excellence: How to Deliver Value to Today's Busy Customer*

For more information, please visit the website:
www.millionpoundmums.com

or scan the QR code below

CHAPTER FIFTEEN

SUCCEED ONLINE

Every business has to be online. No ifs buts or maybes. The first thing anyone does these days is try to find you on Google. You need a website, even if you don't sell online. It can be a full-blown e-commerce site or a one-page information site. Websites can be expensive or cost you very little, it depends entirely on what you need your website for and what you want it to do.

But there are certain fundamentals you have to get right no matter what kind of site you have. Think about how you surf the web, you want the sites you visit to be as easy to use as possible don't you? You may be horribly embarrassed by your children and their ability to navigate things that still leave you scratching your head. Well you don't want your customer scratching his or her head when trying to navigate your site.

The best sites all have the following in common.

Easy to find

Without being easy to find, your website is as much use as a chocolate teapot. No visitors, no sales. Avoid domain names that have symbols or hyphens or names that are too close to another business.

I'll discuss Search Engine Optimisation in a moment, as that deserves some serious consideration all on its own.

Easy to use

Don't clutter it with lots of fancy bits that will bewilder the users when they find you. Have a look at your competitors' sites and see which ones are easiest to use and work out why. Bear in mind not all your customers may have perfect vision so don't make the design hard to read, for instance white writing on a black background is very hard to read for most people. Don't be tempted to put music on it that plays as soon as you open the site. People surf the net in work, they don't want to be caught out!

Make the navigation of your site easy. Look at your favourite websites and see what navigation works. People expect certain pages to be easy to find, like Home, Content, About Us, and My Account. Make it easy for people to move around.

Fast

We are all time-poor and we have less and less patience. If your site takes time to download, your potential customer will be off. Remember your competitor's site is just one click away. Avoid animation or graphics and music unless they're crucial to your product. They take time to download and your customers aren't there to be entertained, they're there to find what they want to buy.

Compatible and consistent

Just because your site can be viewed in Internet Explorer doesn't mean it will appear the same in Firefox. Web browsers are different and your site needs to look good on all of them. Make sure you web designer doesn't just check it in his favourite browser.

Free content

A site that has lots of useful content on it will keep your prospect on your site and they will feel the site is beneficial to them. If you sell skin care, you may want to have a blog on the site on all the latest news in skincare, or a downloadable guide to a good daily skincare routine.

Join up

You want your visitors to feel attached to your site so create a newsletter with good, fresh content, then ask your visitors to sign up to it. It's a good way to capture their email addresses. Get autoresponder software, that's a system that lets you track and keep in touch with your email database very easily. They'll value the content of the newsletter and they will start to trust you. You can then send them special offers and slowly turn them into customers. All it takes is for you to write good content regularly and press Send!

Good links

Providing links to other websites that have information the customer wants can be a real benefit to them. But before you say '...but that takes them away from my site...', make sure to tell your web designer to have that link 'Open in a New Window', that means that they don't navigate away from your site, and when they close that window, they are still with you.

Creating a site

> *"Online, you have about three seconds to make an impression. It doesn't matter if the product is good, if it doesn't look good I'll overlook it."*
>
> Nicola Sankey, Founder of Choose Nutrition

Now you know what type of site you want, you have to create it. There are lots of good templates you can buy now, but hiring a professional can make all the difference between an amateur-looking site and a really slick one. But how do you find the right company to build your site? Well you ask some basic questions.

- See what other sites like yours they have designed and ask to speak to those clients. If they don't let you speak to them they probably have something to hide
- Do they understand what you are trying to achieve, do they have sympathy with your business vision?
- Make sure you can add your own content and edit it, and that you can do it easily. Get them to show you how you can achieve that before you commit to them
- How much will it cost to maintain the site once it's up and running?

Web design and development

Remember there's a difference between a designer and a developer. The designer designs the look and feel of the

155

website, the developer creates the 'back end' with coding, which will determine how the site works which is crucial for making the site effective. You may already be a dab hand with Adobe or Photoshop or know someone who is. Don't be afraid to take your designs to a developer and see what they can do with them. The design element can often be quite expensive.

Search engine optimisation (SEO)

I mentioned SEO earlier and it's worth looking at in a little more detail as it's what will help drive traffic to your website, so it's crucial to your business.

SEO is the process by which you encourage search engines to list your website above your rivals when someone searches for a product you sell.

Everyone wants to be in the top ten, that is, on the first page of Google. How many pages do you go down if you are searching? I'm willing to bet you don't get much past the first page and hardly ever get to page 3.

So how do you get to be listed so high that people will come flocking to your website?

Your domain name

First things first, if your company and your domain name is one that 'does what it says on the tin', that is, describes what you do or sell, you stand a better chance. That's because the words people use to search, the keywords, are likely to be in the name. If your domain name is www.workoveralls.com then obviously you're going to come up pretty high when people search for that. But your domain name doesn't have to be the same as your company name. B&Q's domain name is www.diy.com .

You can buy several domain names and have them all 'pointing' towards your site. Make sure you buy all the main versions of that domain name e.g. .com, .co.uk and .net, or your competitors may well grab the others and benefit from all your hard work.

Key words and phrases

If people are searching for something in particular like 'low cost lamps' then that phrase needs to be in your web copy. But you can't just hurl in lots of phrases hoping the search engine robots will pick them up. They have to make sense. So write your copy carefully so it reads well to humans and to the Google-bots that scurry from site to site looking for keywords and phrases before they rank those sites.

Meta tags

These are words that describe each page in HTML code and they are invisible on your site. They used to be very important, but now less so. But it is still worth adding them.

Links

If other sites link to yours then the search engines 'value' your site more highly, so the more inbound links you can get the better. Be careful though, if you just find other sites and you link to each other to help each other out, that won't help. The search engines interpret these reciprocal links as cheating.

To .com or not to .com?

If you are based in the UK and so are most of your customers then you are better off with a co.uk than a .com Although you should buy the .com and point it at your site to make sure you catch people who aren't certain what you are, and to stop someone stealing your domain name.

Site map

If you have ever wondered what on earth a site map is for, as many do, it helps the search engines to catalogue your site.

Words and pictures

You may be very graphically minded and think that a picture speaks a thousand words, but search engines don't understand pictures. So make sure you add descriptive captions to your pictures and graphics.

Web hosting

Once your site is built, it needs to be hosted. You can either have it hosted on a shared server or a dedicated one. A shared server is cheaper and is fine if your site has low traffic. But if you are expecting thousands of visitors a day or every week then you should pay for a dedicated server. You must find a good host! Spend time chatting to other businesses about who they use and what their experience is. If your site goes down for a day, it could cost you thousands.

TOP TIPS

When writing your web copy …

Use 'you' not 'we', and try to make things sound more personal.

Instead of *'We offer these shoes in 5 colours'* or *'These are available in 5 colours'* you might want to try *'You can choose one of these 5 colours!'*

Keep your text chunks short and easy to read and make sure there's a call to action - put your 'Buy Now' button where the customer can see it easily.

Measure your results

You need to be able to measure how many 'unique visitors' visit your site. This is more important than how many hits you get, as many of those hits will be produced by the same person. You also need to be able to see what each visitor looks at when they're on your site, which pages they go to, how long they spend on those pages and which products they focus on. It will help you to get an idea which pages and products get the best response.

Once you have an idea of your average customer's behaviour on the site you can tailor what you're offering.

You can then create special offers or fix things that people reject or aren't interested in. Think of it like watching a customer in an actual shop. If you had a real-world shop you could see what they browsed, what they picked up and what they ignored. You could ask them how they found your shop, were they passing or were they recommended?

Drive people to your site

SEO alone won't get enough people to your site, not unless you have a niche market in selling a product that no-one else in the world is selling.

So you need to find as many ways as possible to put your website in front of people. These are ways you can build your audience and get more people to discover your site and of course your products. Before we get onto the subject of Social Media, don't forget you can drive traffic to you site from the real world. If you go to events hand out flyers with your website address and a special offer on it, or perhaps a promotional code which gives that person a special deal.

Once you go online, you can use blogs and forums to increase your range. As well as writing your own blog you can add comments to other people's blogs in the relevant area. Or you can take part in discussion groups and forums.

If people like what you say and respect your opinion there is a good chance they will click on your website link.

Social media

But of course one of the best ways to get in front of people is social media. It has revolutionised marketing for small businesses but only if they get it right.

Social media is free to use and you may already use Facebook, Twitter and Pinterest for social reasons. But using social media for business is a whole other ball game. Many business owners make the mistake of thinking that because it is free, they will be able to use it effectively.

Some companies employ a person specifically to focus on social media so don't underestimate how much time it takes, or how well you have to plan a campaign. There are many marketing companies who can help you with this. It is a cost, but it may be worth it, especially if you don't know your Twitter from your Tumblr, or your Facebook from your Flickr. If it drives traffic to your site then it's worth the expenditure.

But if you can't afford that just yet then here are some do's and don'ts

Channel your efforts

It's crucial to think about which of the main networks you should choose to use and how you approach them. Let's look at the four most popular channels – Twitter, Facebook, Linkedin and Google+. What's the difference?

This is what online social media hub Mashable.com has to say…

Twitter – should be seen as conversational and quickfire – the place to get bites of the latest company news, personal insights from you, the business leader, and responses to customer queries.

Facebook – is about sharing, community and involvement – so use it to post links to presentations, photos of new products, invitations to events and special offers. You can also use it to ask customers questions useful for research.

LinkedIn – is where you show your professional credentials and should always be up to date.

Google+ – Segments people into groups by their interests and targets them with relevant information.

So should you open lots of accounts? No you shouldn't!

DON'T open too many accounts. If you do that, inevitably some of them will lie dormant and abandoned and that's not what you want your customers to see. You will look like you are hardly doing business. However because our books range from cooking to erotica we do have a number of Facebook pages so as not to confuse or upset our customers.

"Don't say anything online that you wouldn't want plastered on a billboard with your face on it."

Erin Bury, Community Manager, Sprouter

Respond to people

Once you open a channel you have to respond to comments and correspondence and do it consistently. It will impress existing and potential customers. Don't be slow to respond and don't ignore people.

But don't just answer when you have to. You have an opportunity, to surprise with a message which demonstrates that the brand is out there alive and kicking. But keep it reasonable. Resist the temptation to over-exploit this direct line to your customers. Chasing followers makes you look desperate. If you provide good content and a discussion that makes people want to join in, then they will. Social media space is not brand space, a person's Facebook page is their world, so think carefully how you tread in their space.

Get help

Research shows that many Facebook users are more likely to become a fan of a brand if they see a family member or friend is a fan. So encouraging your existing followers to recommend you by giving you a 'like' or sharing a link is a useful tactic. But don't confuse 'likes' with customers. What you are looking for here is traction and spreading the word. And don't expect people to recommend you for nothing. People are conscious now of their potential to influence how a brand is doing. Try offering incentives like a discount for giving you a 'like', or sharing a particular product link. We use a great website called www.shortstack.com for building Facebook apps that engage people with giveaways and games.

Look for opinions

Social media is a great way to get feedback, but don't just look at the good feedback, look for the bad, and the gaps in what you're offering. Make time to read what your followers are talking about. If you find someone saying 'I love their shoes but I wish they made them in half sizes" and lots of people are agreeing, then that tells you that you might be missing potential sales.

Consistency

You also need to make sure your message is consistent across all platforms. You don't want one personality on Twitter and a completely different one on Facebook.

Staffing your social media

You can't start a social media campaign and then disappear. So if you can't staff it yourself, then outsource it or take someone on. But remember you have to give anyone who operates your social media accounts very clear guidance on what they can and can't say. Twitter comments can go viral all too quickly. You should never say anything you wouldn't be happy seeing on the front page of a newspaper or headlining the 10 o'clock news. It is a public space even though it feels private. And once something is on the internet, it's there FOREVER!

Apps, widgets and tools

A simple Google search can find you an endless array of free, quickly downloadable interactive elements to add to your sites – from voting polls to shopping baskets. This can skyrocket your following if you are providing a widget that makes the customer's life easier or more fun.

Measure everything

You need to know if your social media campaign is effective. So you need to decide what you want to achieve and then measure it. You can get user-friendly social media dashboards like HootSuite to track the activity on all your social media sites at once. It's easy, accessible and very importantly not hugely time-consuming.

Be patient

We all want rapid returns and we want to know that whatever we are doing is effective. But you have to have a little patience with a social media campaign and be prepared to throw some money at it. It's not about rapid returns it's about building relationships.

Don't get upset

It's inevitable that when you open yourself up to customer opinions you will get negative comments. Research by TOA Technologies claims that 80% of customer service tweets are negative. But remember people have a tendency to use social media for gripes, so don't let it put you off.

Selling online

So now you've got people to your site. But you have a few more things to do before you can guarantee they will click 'Place Order' and enter their credit card details.

We'll take it as read that you have created a really good, professional-looking website that has inspired confidence in your potential customers. They also need to be confident their financial details are safe.

Secure payments

Your bank should provide you with merchant services to enable you to take credit card payments securely. If you want to set it up more simply sites like Paypal and Worldpay are a good alternative. Although be careful as some of these payment sites hang on to your money for a while, so check out the terms and conditions before you choose.

Fast buying

Make sure the buying process takes as few clicks as possible. You don't want them getting fed up half way through paying and give up. If they lose patience, you lose a sale, so don't overcomplicate the buying process. Offering accounts is a good way to make the buying process easier. If you buy from Amazon you will be familiar with their 'Buy with 1 Click' option. If you offer accounts that store people's data, make sure you conform to data protection regulations.

The Act contains eight Data Protection Principles.

The data must be:

- Processed fairly and lawfully

- Obtained and used only for specified and lawful purposes

- Adequate, relevant and not excessive

- Accurate, and where necessary, kept up to date

- Kept for no longer than necessary

- Processed in accordance with the individual's rights

- Kept secure

- Transferred only to countries that offer adequate data protection

Take advice to make sure that you conform to all the legal requirements regarding data.

Pricing

Prices have to be visible. No-one wants to get all excited about a product after reading all the specs and reviews then have to hunt for the price and find it's too much. You'll annoy your customer and they won't come back.

Support

Most customers trust websites that have a phone number they can call if things go wrong. If you are a one-woman-band, then consider a telephone answering service. They can tell customers that the customer service is team is busy and take a number. If you get back to them quickly and answer their query or sort out a problem you'll keep the customer.

Comparison

Adding an 'If you like that you'll like this' option greatly increases your chances of getting a larger sale. Customers may come to your site unaware of your range. They're looking for one thing and you've just made it easier for them to choose a second product. Selling two products to one customer is far more effective than selling one product each to two customers. Each customer costs you money to get, in time and marketing, so the more one of them spends the better.

Stay in touch

Once they've placed an order, customers should get an email detailing their order and giving them a reference. Keep them informed about dispatch and delivery.

For more information, please visit the website:
www.millionpoundmums.com

or scan the QR code below

CHAPTER SIXTEEN

CONTROLLING YOUR CASH FLOW

> *"That cash-flow is key. If your cash flow is failing or thriving, that's the indicator for the success of your business."*
>
> Caroline Sparks, Founder and Director of Turtle Tots

Cash flow is king. It's one of the oldest clichés in business but it's a cliché for a reason, and that's because it's absolutely true. If you've never run a business sometimes it's hard to see why it's so important. But just imagine, if there isn't enough money in the business at any given time, none can go out. So if you have to order stock to fulfil customer requests but not enough money has come in to cover the cost, you're stuck.

Cash flow is the blood that keeps the heart of your company pumping. It's one of the most critical components for a small or mid-sized business. Big companies can have sophisticated in-house credit management teams to help them, but small companies are usually so focused on running the business day-to-day, that they forget to keep a close eye on cash flow.

If you don't exercise good cash management you may not be able to make the investments you need to compete, or you may have to pay more to borrow money to function.

To get a grip on your cash flow ask yourself these two questions.

1. What is my cash balance right now?

2. What do I expect my cash balance to be six months from now?

If you can't answer these two questions, then strap yourself in for a wild ride on that rollercoaster, because it's about to get really scary. You don't have your cash flow under control!

TOP TIP

You should be tracking cash flow, either weekly, monthly or quarterly. But track it you must.

There are essentially two kinds of cash flow:

Positive cash flow

This is when the cash funnelling into your business from sales and accounts receivable is more than the amount of the cash leaving your businesses through accounts payable, monthly expenses, salaries and so on.

Negative cash flow

This happens when the cash going out is more than the cash coming in. This usually spells trouble, but there are steps you can take to generate or collect more cash while maintaining or cutting your expenses.

Positive cash flow doesn't happen by accident. You have to work at it. Most accounting software packages geared to small or mid-sized businesses – such as Quickbooks or Sage – will help you produce a cash flow statement. There are also other websites offering free templates.

Profit versus cash flow

Profit doesn't equal cash flow. You can't just look at your profit and loss statement, or P & L as it's known, to get a grip on your cash flow.

Lots of other figures feed into factoring your cash flow, including accounts receivable, inventory, accounts payable, capital expenditures, and debt service.

Smart cash-flow management requires a laser focus on each of these drivers of cash, in addition to your profit or loss. Profit is simply revenue minus expenses. Invoicing a customer for products or services generates revenue. But actually collecting the money on that invoice is what creates cash.

You need a positive cash flow to generate profits. You need enough cash to pay your employees and suppliers so that you can make or buy goods. You sell those goods to generate a profit. But if you don't have the money to make the goods, you don't end up with the profit.

How to improve cash flow

Consolidate predictables

Every business has core monthly bills that include things like rent, payroll, and telephone service that are consistent and predictable. Consolidate these numbers into one operating expense figure that reflects how much cash must come in the door every month to stay in business. If you have a negative cash flow, this is known as a burn rate. You need to know the burn rate in your new business, and managing it well will tell you, and any investors, when you'll need more investment or a loan, or when you'll break even and begin to make a profit.

If you forget to check this barometer, you could run out of cash before you reach those milestones, and you'll find your business is burnt out, completely!

Invoice promptly

As soon as you've finished a job send your customer the bill. Make sending the invoice part of the job in your head. Don't wait until the end of the week or the month to invoice. You'll probably have to give them 30 days to pay, or whatever payments terms you've agreed, so the sooner you invoice the better. You'll already be a month behind even if the customer pays on time.

These days it is not unusual to ask for a percentage to be paid with the order – for example, when we had a new computer system installed recently we had to pay 50% when ordering and the other 50% when the installation was complete. Consider if you can do this with your business, or if there is a way you can offer a subscription or repeat business model that will help your cash flow. I get my nails done on a very regular basis – if the salon offered me a free manicure for purchasing a voucher for five manicures, I would probably go for it. They'd have the money up front, I'd feel I'd got a bargain and there is always the chance I wouldn't redeem so they'd be quids-in.

Get paid on time

If your customers are other businesses then you might have to chase payments. Large companies can be particularly bad at paying on time because they're large and have a lot of processing to do. Small companies may pay late either because they're disorganised or they're trying to manage their own cash flow! Don't be afraid to make a polite phone call when time is up.

Pay slowly

Just as some businesses may pay you slowly because they're hanging on to their cash, you too can pay slowly. You will have to be careful that you don't annoy companies you depend on though. Don't pay late, but pay as late as you can while still sticking to their payment terms. If they give you 30 days to pay, then pay on Day 29 not Day 9.

Tighten credit requirements

Businesses often have to extend credit to other businesses who are customers, particularly when starting out or growing. But you have to do your research beforehand to determine the risk of extending credit to each customer. Can they pay their bills on time? Is their business growing or faltering? Are they having cash-flow problems?

Increasing sales

If you need more cash, it seems like a no-brainer to go out and try to attract new customers or sell more goods or services to your existing customers. If you have existing customers could you send them out a special offer by email? But I must sound one word of caution: you may just increase your accounts receivables and not actual cash if these sales are on credit.

Spend less

This is another no-brainer. The less you spend the more cash you'll have. Look at where you can cut costs even if those cuts are only temporary until your cash flow improves.

Pricing discounts

One option is to offer your customers discounts if they pay early. This may hit your profit margin, but it may help your cash flow by giving your customers an incentive to pay up earlier than they normally would.

Buying stock when you need to

Buying things just before you need them means you aren't carrying stock. If your business can sustain this and you can still get orders out to customers in good time, it's worth trying. One lesson I have learned the hard way is not to tie cash up in stock. Our unit cost is much lower if we print 3000 books than 300 but ONLY IF WE SELL THEM! If they languish in the warehouse attracting storage costs, then they cost far more in the long run.

Keep your stock levels as low as possible and avoid the temptation to buy extra stock because it's discounted. One of the major reasons businesses fail is because they are overstocked and crippled by lack of cash flow.

Have a sale

Get rid of old stock that isn't shifting quickly enough. You may lose some margin, but your cash flow will be healthier and you can keep the business moving.

TOP TIP

Remember those old pirate movies where the salty old sea dog bites a gold coin to check that it's real before he accepts it? Well modern business is no different. A deal is just a giant I.O.U until the cash is in your hands.

Avoid direct debits

Direct debits are wonderful if you hate having to be organised enough to pay bills. But it also means you don't control when you pay people. Try to be organised enough to pay your bills when you should, but still retain the ability to pay when it suits you, and not when it suits other people.

Secure a loan

Short-term cash flow problems may sometimes mean you need to take a loan out or secure a bigger overdraft. Even though the interest on a loan or the payment needed to secure a larger overdraft are an expense for your business, sometimes it's the difference between carrying on trading or coming to a grinding halt. Your bank manager should work with you to manage your cash flow. When you sign up with a business bank they should analyse what your needs are and re-assess them as your business grows.

Adjust for growth

It's critically important to account for the capital your company needs to grow. Too many successful businesses fail because they didn't have enough cash to fund their growth. New sales often mean you'll need to spend more money on equipment, employees, and marketing. In most cases, the expenses come before the sale which means you need the cash available in advance.

When cash flow gets harder

There are times when you have to keep an even closer eye on your cash flow than normal. Things can change for the worst very quickly, so pay attention in these situations:

In the beginning

When you start a business you will always have more costs than you planned. When you get into a routine it will be easier, but to begin with you'll probably be all over the place. Your bank manager should help you to assess what you need when you begin business banking.

In a recession

Everyone has less money and everyone hangs onto that money longer. So you may find it harder to get paid and your outgoings seem to speed up in comparison with your income. There is also a much higher risk of your customers folding – can your business survive if your debtors default?

Seasonally

At Christmas and in January you have to watch your income. Many companies' accounts departments have people on leave and some close down over Christmas, making it hard to get paid. Then come January, everyone's credit card bills start landing on the doorstep with a thud. And if you're trying to get money out of someone who is self-employed, remember that they will have a tax bill to pay at the end of January. So the end of one year and the beginning of the next can be a tight squeeze.

Competition

If a new competitor appears, or existing competitors decide to undercut you, then you may have to spend to win or keep customers, and that will hit your margins and cash flow.

Illness or holiday

If you are a one-woman band, then any time you take away from the business could mean a slow-down in income, but probably not in your costs. If you have decided to work from home then your outgoings shouldn't be huge, but if you have premises all the bills still need to be paid.

Weather

Torrential rain or heavy snow can keep customers from coming into your shop or driving to your premises. And if you sell wet weather clothing, you aren't going to do a roaring trade if we get a blazing hot summer. I know that doesn't happen often but it does happen! So plan for the seasons if they affect your trade.

Get a 'crystal ball'

No, not a real one, but the spreadsheet version! You should be able to see danger points coming if you have planned properly. Keep looking several months ahead and plan accordingly.

VAT

VAT can easily get lost in your cash flow. But it can cause real problems when your VAT quarter comes around. HMRC do not take kindly to late payments and can fine you heavily.

If you are going to have trouble talk to them, they sometimes allow deferred payments. But if you don't talk to them then you can guarantee you won't get much sympathy. Plan for VAT payments.

Talk to suppliers

When you hit a wall with cash flow you may be able to get goods on account if you have a good relationship with your suppliers. Try to establish a good relationship from the outset and they'll be more tolerant when you ask for extra time to pay. They may not allow you credit on a complete order but they may allow you to pay 50% up front and 50% later. This can make accounting a bit of a nightmare but it's better than losing an order because you can't pay for the goods.

Early warning

Have a warning system in place so that you find out in time if you are heading into the red.

For more information, please visit the website:
www.millionpoundmums.com

or scan the QR code below

CHAPTER SEVENTEEN

MANAGE AND GROW

There comes a point in your business where things are running smoothly, or relatively smoothly but you know you could do more. It's time to capitalise on your success so far. Your kids are growing, so is it time to grow your business too?

Kids never stop growing, you turn your back and they've shot up a couple of inches and now those trousers you bought last month are already too small! Well, your business must grow too, you can't rest on your laurels. Things change, your competitors might have started noticing you so you have to keep moving, keep evolving.

But how? In which direction?

You may find you have no choice but to grow because your business is doing well and you can't cope all on your own. If that's the case it's time to take on staff. Many small businesses will start as a one-woman outfit and the idea of employing and managing people can be scary. But how do you know when it's time to take on staff, or if you already have some, when to take on more?

Here are a few things that should alert you to the need for more people in your company.

If your employees are complaining that they have too much to do, then listen. Now complaints like this are common and your task is deciding whether it's a legitimate complaint or whether they're just whinging.

How can you do that? Try talking to your employees and asking them to validate their concerns of being 'overworked'. Then look at any patterns in attendance and productivity to see if their claim stacks up. If what you find confirms what they're saying, and they are doing too much, then you might decide to reorganize and restructure their roles and responsibilities so they can deal with the workflow better. Or you could decide it's time to hire more people

Is it time to hire more staff?

Every business is different but some of the following might provide a trigger for putting that ad in the Situations Vacant page or finding a recruiter.

- Up until now you may have done everything on your own and you're reluctant to let go of the reins and find someone you can delegate tasks to. But remember why you started the business in the first place, because you wanted to be there for your kids and have more control over your life. Don't lose sight of that. I employed my first person within three months of starting Accent Press. I'd finish at three and go and get the kids from school but she'd keep the office running until 5.30. It was a great decision as it enabled me to relax and enjoy the kids knowing that the business was still being cared for

- You see an opportunity to expand but aren't sure if you can cope if you do expand

- If you have employees already, and you realise that their existing job skills and knowledge are fine for what your company is doing now but they don't have the skills you need for expansion, you'll either need to increase their skills and knowledge by paying for training, or hire a new person who has those skills

- You're making more money than you thought. Do you bank it and throw a party, or think about hiring staff that will help you expand?

Any of these should alert you to the fact that it may be time to start hiring. If you are planning to recruit, it is worth checking if there are any government schemes in place to help fund your new staff. We have benefitted from a couple that are aimed at getting young people work placements.

Managing people

We've already looked at how to find the right people, now I want to talk about how to manage them. Growth depends on your team.

To really grow a business you need to focus not just on how your staff behave but on how you behave. Manage people well and your business stands a much better chance of flourishing.

Taking people on is just the start. Once they work for you, they expect direction from you and to be managed by you.

For most businesses wages are the biggest cost, so you

have to get it right. Focus on being the best boss you can be if you want to get the best out of your staff.

You will probably know only too well what it's like to work for tyrants or idiots. They seem to rise to the top in so many industries. You always thought "I could do better than that!" and now you have started a business you have the chance to prove it.

But how?

We've all met the tyrannical boss who creates an "Us and Them" atmosphere, or the stressed-out boss who never has time for you or your concerns. What type of boss would you like to be?

TOP TIP

Don't just manage your staff, be a leader. They want to feel there is someone at the helm who knows where they are going, especially in a small firm. You company is embryonic and still growing, so they may worry about job security. So think like an army officer, never show fear and always lead from the front.

Good management is about valuing people, getting the most from them and leading them.

The four key things to remember are:

- Be Flexible. Life is never black or white, or made in straight lines. If you are flexible then your staff will find working for you much easier

- Get to know each member of your staff as a person, not just as a body you hired to do the filing or the accounts. If you want them to stay with you, stay loyal and give you 100%, then they have to feel you are invested in them

- Praise them when they do well and encourage them. It's too easy to tell them when something has gone wrong and forget to tell them they've done something well. Make sure you notice when they're doing well

- Communicate your vision to them. They can't fall in line with your vision for the company if they don't really know what it is

"I think if staff are proud and thrilled with the company it bleeds down into the consumers. So finding a way to have a sense of protecting the family is what companies should be doing."

Anita Roddick, Founder, The Body Shop

My first member of staff, Rachel, gave me an idea that got me my first distribution deal for my publishing company. I went from being a tiny company with only 5 titles to getting a distribution deal with Macmillan who are huge and usually only take on larger publishers. And it all happened because I listened to my one and only staff member. So encourage your staff to come up with ideas and try them. Then reward them if they work.

It's very easy to stop listening when you're frantically busy running a new company, but listen to your staff. Have an open-door policy, make sure they can talk to you whenever they need to.

Even though you must listen to your staff, praise them and be flexible you still need to show who's boss. If they aren't pulling their weight you have to show them. It doesn't have to be confrontational. You can ask them if they are having problems and talk about how to address them. They won't feel you are finding fault and might pull their socks up. Everyone makes mistakes and you have to allow for a few. If they don't and are just plain lazy then you must have a firm hand.

> *"It's a danger when you start a company that you become a lynchpin. You have to leave in order for other people to step up. But it takes a strong person to know what to delegate and what to leave."*
>
> Debbie Taylor, Founder and Editorial Director of *Mslexia*

You can't do everything yourself and that's why you employed staff, so learn to delegate properly. You have to let go of a task if you give it to someone else, and trust that they will do it. No-one likes working for a micro-manager. If you empower people they will usually become more responsible and live up to the trust you have put in them.

Create milestones, and when you reach them celebrate with your staff and let them know they helped you get there.

Here are some great extra tips on how to be motivational to your staff

A happy home – Create a nice environment. It doesn't have to be a designer office, but no-one wants to work in a dark brown room with peeling wallpaper. And keep it clean – no one wants to use a smelly loo or a microwave in a kitchen that's almost a nuclear hazard, it's so dirty!

Celebrate together – Make a note of everyone's birthdays and buy cakes. Or create special days like the last Friday of the month, when you do something different or special. Create little competitions like hitting a target, without it being a form of pressure. If there are fun prizes then it won't feel like you are breathing down their necks. Prizes really don't have to be expensive, and they don't necessarily have to be something people keep. You could create a 'baton' that gets passed on from week to week like a wooden spoon or a comedy trophy.

Be flexible – You wanted to work for yourself because you were tired of being tied to a workplace. Well, your employees probably feel tied too. So think about flexible working or annualised hours. If you can accommodate their work-life balance better than most employers, you'll get their loyalty and they'll stay with you.

Charities and causes – If your employees have a cause that's close to their hearts, you might want to support it, even if it's for a month or six months. They will feel appreciated and it has the added benefit that it might get you noticed by other people who support it too, and they could be potential customers. Give some of your products away in a raffle or sponsor a charity event.

TOP TIP

Team prizes that combine humour with public recognition will go down well. You could create one prize like giving the best salesperson that month a magic wand!

Have hot drinks – Make sure you supply drinks and don't make them pay for the supplies. Tea and coffee keep us going through the day. You'd be amazed by how appreciated the odd packet of Kit Kats is too!

Have a team outing – If you can't afford an away day, a simple team drink after work or a Friday lunch can work wonders for team-building.

Give them good titles – Having a prestige title can mean all the difference to someone's self-esteem. Account Director sounds much grander than Salesperson.

Being a mum and a manager

If you have left a job, either as a worker or a manager, you will know how important it is to be able to balance work and family. And if you are taking on female employees you will know that they probably have the same concerns. I've talked about being flexible and letting your workers know that you understand their concerns but it's very easy as a woman to forget to put the correct amount of emotional distance between you and your workers.

Women very often don't know what kind of boss they should be. We've all met the Ice Queen boss. They think they have to behave in a stand-offish kind of way to show their authority. They don't take much interest in their employees' hopes and dreams. And they certainly don't encourage fun and laughter. They manage emotional distance, but by keeping their employees at more than arm's length. This is counter-productive, particularly in a small firm. People want to work where they are known and valued, and they give more when they are.

By contrast, many women who've suffered at the hands of a bad boss want to adopt a more motherly approach. But they make a mistake that many women make and that's to blur the line between boss and friend. That can be great while everything is going well, but what if you have to ask them to do something difficult or deliver a tough message about their performance? Then your close relationship can backfire spectacularly, with your employee feeling hurt or betrayed.

Finding the right emotional distance so you can motivate your staff and make them feel you value them, and being at enough of a distance that they know you are the boss and it's your company, that's the trick. Not easy I know, but you should try and strike the right balance from the beginning, as it will be very difficult to correct once your company starts to evolve its own culture.

Another difficulty many women bosses have is being too generous in an attempt to create a workplace unlike any of the bad ones they may have suffered in the past.

> *"Handling emotional distances is one of the most complex challenges a boss faces, male or female. But the Ice Queen and Good Mother leadership styles, both so common, make doing it all the harder. The remedy lies in striking the right intimacy balance – close enough to know your people, distant enough to lead them."*
>
> Suzy Welch, Author, Commentator and Business Journalist

I spoke to another business woman some time ago who ran a small firm with about 10 staff. She told me she looked after her staff really well with parties for birthdays, babies, and marriages and she took a real interest in each individual. But instead of being grateful they still complained all the time! She was at her wits' end because nothing seemed to make them happy.

The complaint will sound very familiar to a lot of female bosses. Many of them set out to create kinder workplaces, only to find themselves the victims of their own kindness. Be good to your staff but don't go overboard or there's a danger you will be basically training them to ask for more and more and more. You don't want to create a culture of entitlement where your employees focus on what your company can do for them, forgetting what they should be doing for your company. You want them focused on serving customers, finding new opportunities to grow and making money for the company.

If you find yourself in this situation, then it's time for a frank conversation about what the company is all about. You may of course have to let people go once you have hired them.

Another mistake many women bosses make is to hang on to people too long when they're not up to the job, or not playing the game. They tend to avoid confrontation and worry about the employee and her family. If you're a mum you might feel too much sympathy for your employee who's a mum. So women often try to coach and cajole the employee more, they may even change the job description to make it easier for them so that it works. But this can have a knock-on effect on the rest of the team who have to take up the slack.

So how do you handle this? Know how to keep your professional and personal relationships apart. Socialise and listen to your staff, but make sure your staff don't see you as a soft touch.

Written policies are rare in small firms but it is always best to set out parameters for your staff. If you are growing your company you don't suddenly want to have to retro-fit these policies once your staff have got used to a certain way of doing things. If you have a flexible working policy make sure your staff know how flexible it is and where it is not flexible. If you have birthday parties in the office or time for tea and cake make sure they all know when party time is over and it's time to get back to work. Or nominate who will answer the phones whilst you are all tucking in to chocolate cake and fizz. You don't have to be heavy-handed. Just ask some work questions and show that you are going back to work. Perhaps ask to discuss something with one of the people in the group. People respond to a change of tone and body language. You will show that you care about them as people but also show that they are part of a business, your business and they have responsibilities as well as privileges.

Every business is different and every business culture is different. Talk to other women entrepreneurs about how they handle their staff and the problems they've had. Everyone makes mistakes and you might as well learn from other people's mistakes as your own. Get yourself mentors. Not just one, but many, who will all be able to teach you different things. It will help you learn and it will help you let off steam with someone who understands your problems.

For more information, please visit the website:
www.millionpoundmums.com

or scan the QR code below

CHAPTER EIGHTEEN

MENTORS

The former chairman of ICI, John Harvey-Jones, helped lots of businesses when he appeared in the BBC series 'Troubleshooter' in the 1990s. His advice was very often controversial, but when someone asked him what gave him the right to tell other people how to run their business, he said it was because he'd make every damned mistake in the book and he'd made it twice!

Mentors will make an enormous difference to you and your company because they'll be giving you advice from the trenches, they've probably been where you are and they know how to cope with the problems you are facing.

They'll also help you to realise that getting things wrong is OK, mistakes are not disasters. This back-up will be invaluable to you as go through the highs and lows of running your business. Very often it's the smallest piece of advice that someone gives you, perhaps just the smallest tip, which will make a huge difference to how you do things.

Not everyone has access to a man like John Harvey-Jones, who'd run one of the world's most famous multi-national companies, but you have access to mentors, whether you know it or not!

How to find your mentors

Start with family and friends

They are usually the first people we turn to when we have a problem, and most business problems can be resolved with a healthy dose of common sense. So start close to home. But remember you need to be getting advice from someone you will be willing to take advice from. And you may find that your friends and family give you enough unsolicited advice already and you'd like some solicited advice!

Your extended network

It is good to find a mentor who doesn't know you as well as your family does. But how do you ask for such a big commitment from a near stranger? Reach out to your network of contacts. Get a friend or a colleague to refer you, as a positive word from a mutual friend can go a long way towards getting a mentoring relationship off to a good start. Or you may want to take your time and wait until you meet your potential mentor in person before asking to pick their brains. Successful people are often very generous with their advice. They had to come up the hard way and they'll know how valuable good advice is. People like sharing war stories!

Beyond your network

But perhaps no-one in any of your networks is the right person for you. So start doing some research and look for the people you would like to become your mentor. Look for someone who matches your style or your way of thinking. But you can't just march in and ask them. Contact them and see if you can schedule a quick phone call to pick their brains on a specific subject. They may say no but you may be surprised. They may be flattered that you consider their opinion is worth something. If they will see you in person then make sure you travel to them. Make it as easy as possible for them to help you. If it goes well, you can broach the subject of possibly contacting them again. They may even suggest that you can call them should you hit a snag.

Look to your competitors

Obviously I don't mean your direct competition. But you could talk to someone who sells in your field but not in your niche, or you could contact someone who does what you do but in another part of the country. Be careful with contacting someone who sells exactly what you sell though, as the internet now means businesses hundreds of miles apart are competing for the same people.

Find a mentoring organisation

There are organisations which work to find mentors for small businesses. Very often they are attached to universities or business networks. Many will work to find women mentors to help other women.

Talk to your bank

Many banks either offer mentoring services or they hold events where they introduce businesses to each other that they think will be mutually beneficial. Talk to your bank manager about the possibility of mentoring.

Look to your industry

Many trade organisation and their publications are good places to look for potential mentors. You might also find that suppliers and distributors are very useful as they understand your business problems.

Pay for a mentor

You may not have time to build relationships, you may need advice now. You might need to hire a consultant for a short period. Make sure you get recommendations and check to see what kind of businesses they have helped in the past to see if they will understand your business and have been successful for their other clients.

For more information, please visit the website:
www.millionpoundmums.com

or scan the QR code below

CHAPTER NINETEEN

COPING WITH THE UNEXPECTED

No matter how much you plan, or how many to-do lists you draw up you will always be caught out by things you don't expect. It's very easy to get focussed on things because they feel like an emergency and take your eye off your main priority, which is to build your business. But sometimes you will have to deal with a genuine crisis. You will have to fire-fight, there's no getting around it. The trick is not to let the fires get too big.

Unplanned events can have a devastating effect on small businesses. Anything from a real fire, to stock damage, you or your staff getting ill, or your IT system crashing. All these things could make it difficult or even impossible to carry out your normal day-to-day activities.

You could end up losing customers or worse, going out of business altogether. But with good planning you can take steps to minimise the potential impact of a disaster – and ideally prevent it happening in the first place.

How can I plan for a crisis?

You may be wondering how on earth you can predict the unpredictable but you can put things in place to prevent things going wrong or to stop them ruining your business. There's a number of things you can do:

- Identify potential crises that might affect you

- Work out how you intend to minimise the risks of these disasters happening

- Set out how you'll react if a disaster happens, in a business continuity plan

- Test that plan regularly

If you have a continuity plan it helps you cope and it also proves to investors and customers that you can cope with whatever is thrown at you. It might also give you an edge over your competitors.

So what could hit your business?

Depending on what your business does, there are lots of circumstances that could knock you off kilter.

Natural disasters like flooding caused by burst water pipes or heavy rain, or wind damage after a bad storm.

Theft or vandalism. If someone took one of your computers that could be devastating. Make sure you're insured for loss from theft and install a burglar alarm.

Fire. Make sure if you have premises that you comply with fire regulations and do everything you can to minimise the risks. Make sure all your electrical equipment is regularly tested, and that the batteries in your smoke alarm haven't died. If you can't use your building could you work from rented offices or could you set up an arrangement with another business where you can share their space?

Power cut. If you rely on IT or telecoms what would you do if you couldn't use it?

IT system failure. Are you protected from computer viruses and hackers? Do you have adequate IT back-up? You may want to get a maintenance cover plan that guarantees a fast emergency call-out. You might also consider paying an IT company to back up your data regularly on a secure server offsite. Printing out copies of your customer database can be a good way of making sure you can still contact customers if your IT system fails.

Loss or illness of key staff. How would you cope if there was a flu bug going around that knocked you out or half of your staff? Make sure you know how you'd cope without these important people. Try to make sure you're not dependent on a few staff for key skills by getting them to train other people. You could talk to temping agencies and find one who would be able to send you the right kind of staff. You don't want to be frantically ringing around on the day and risk taking on a temp who is useless to you and expensive. And take health and safety seriously to reduce the risk of staff injuries.

Are you adequately insured? You'll only know this once you assess all the risk factors in your business. For example, if you only have one member of staff and they walk to work, what if you have to make a delivery in your car and you fall ill? Have you insured that employee to drive your car? Do you have insurance that covers you for an employee spilling coffee into their laptop?

Other people's disasters

What about crises that affect the people you do business with? They'll affect you too.

Your suppliers. Have you got alternative suppliers ready to step in, should your existing supplier have a problem?

Customers who can't pay. Have you made sure you have allowed for a sudden crisis affecting a major customer?

Product Recall. Can you save your reputation if one line of products you stock is recalled? Do you have a way to communicate immediately with your customers and who pays for the recall, you or the supplier?

Plan for the unexpected

Even if some of these scenarios seem unlikely, it's wise to give them some thought. Assess the possible impact of risks on your business because it will help you work out what's essential and what isn't. You'll probably find that roles that seem important day to day, aren't absolutely critical if disaster strikes.

Decide which scenarios are low risk and which are high. You may decide you don't need to do anything about a low risk factor, like a terrorist attack, but you do need to consider what to do if your staff all go off sick with the Norovirus.

What about your customers? It's really important to look at what your customers will do if you're affected by crisis. Would they be likely to look elsewhere?

You need to work out whether you would be able to keep to service-level agreements (SLAs) and what the consequences would be if you couldn't.

Contingency plan

You should draw up a business plan setting out in writing how you will cope if a crisis does happen. You need to work out the key business functions you need to get operating as quickly as possible and the resources you'll need. You also need to work out the roles of individuals in the emergency.

Making the most of the first hour after an emergency happens is really important so your plan needs to explain what needs to be done immediately.

It's good idea to arrange the plan in checklists. They're much easier to read when people are flapping in panic!

Include contact details for the people you absolutely have to speak to, people like the emergency services, insurers, customers, suppliers, utility companies.

It's also worth including details of the people who can dig you out of a hole, people like electricians, locksmiths, plumbers and IT specialists. Your staff can't work if the one and only toilet is blocked. You could lose a whole day's trading if you can't get the plumber in quickly, or you will pay through the nose for an emergency plumber!

If your problem is likely to be of interest to the press make sure you know how you will deal with that. Make sure you have a single company spokesperson, which will probably be you and make sure you staff know to refer any enquiries to that person and not to talk to the press. And make sure your staff and customers know first, you don't want them finding out from the press.

Finally, make sure you and key members of your staff have a hard copy of your contingency plan and that you all take a copy home. It won't be much good to you if you keep it in the office and you can't get in!

And remember to update your plan regularly because your business is hopefully growing which means things change. If you move into new premises, you could face an entirely new set of risks.

Let's have a look at some more specific surprises you could be confronted with.

Staff

If you are taking on staff then your business is probably doing well. But taking on living, breathing human beings with all their idiosyncrasies and foibles will be challenging, make no mistake!

Here are some problems to look out for.

Throwing a sickie – People get ill, we all know that, but calling in sick doesn't always mean they are genuinely under the weather. Record sick leave and check for patterns. Make sure your employees know if they have a problem they can come to you and take time off for personal matters if it's urgent. Better than having them throw a sickie with no warning.

Always late – Find out if there's a problem. Perhaps they have childcare issues or they can't fit in the school run and get to you by 9. If they work hard and are an asset you don't want to lose them and they probably feel guilty for being so late, so try changing their start time. On the other hand if someone is always late because they're lazy or they've been out partying then you have to make sure they know it's not acceptable.

Stealing or pilfering – Stealing is a serious issue but most employees will indulge in a spot of pilfering, be it loo paper, pens or Sellotape. If stuff is disappearing too quickly make it harder for people to pilfer. Store the stuff that can too easily walk out the door in a place where they have to get a key to access it. Don't be too dictatorial about it though, you don't want people to feel like they're coming to see the headmistress for a new pen.

Long trips – If your employee runs a business errand or goes on a business trip, do they take too long? Are they combining it with something else, like shopping or paying someone a visit? You have to play this one by ear. If they work hard and get results then you might want to turn a blind eye. It all depends how much time they take out of the working day you are paying them for.

Moonlighting – You may find your employees are doing two jobs. If it doesn't affect your business that's fine. But make sure they aren't compromising your business by working for someone who could be your competitor, or coming in to work exhausted.

Different faiths and values – You may find that one of your employees objects to something you have asked them to do on moral or religious grounds. You have to respect their point of view so adapt.

Clashing egos – If two of your employees just aren't getting on discuss the problem with both of them separately at first, but then you must have a meeting with both of them and agree a solution. Explain your decision and make it clear that the situation isn't acceptable because it harms your business.

Providing a service

If you're a one-woman company providing a service like training, or you're a consultant, you will hit your own set of problems.

Vague instructions – If your client didn't make it clear what they wanted it will be hard to measure whether you've done what they wanted. Make sure you get clear terms of reference that you both agree on and understand.

Over-promising and under-delivering – This is a cardinal sin in business but it's very easy to do when someone comes to you for help. Don't promise to fix everything. Get those terms of reference.

Wrong or unrealistic expectations – Very often clients don't know what they need or they think they know but they're wrong. If you are being hired to do something when you know that isn't their real problem then tell them. If you just do what they ask they'll blame you when it doesn't fix their problem. They might go elsewhere because they don't believe you, but better to keep your reputation intact. You don't want them telling people they hired you and you were useless.

TOP TIP

Don't get overwhelmed worrying about what you can't control and focus on what you can control or what you can plan for.

There's a difference between risk and fear. You can plan for risk because it's usually measurable and manageable. Your fears are often irrational or not useful.

Suppliers and distributors

If you sell products you have to get them to customers. But sometimes you can be doing everything right and the people you rely on at either end of the process can let you down.

Going bust – If you rely too much on one supplier then you are in for trouble if they go to the wall and you haven't got an alternative.

Goods getting lost – Your customers will be furious if they don't get what they ordered. Make sure you employ a really reliable fulfilment company to get your goods to them. You get what you pay for. If the fulfilment company's rates are very cheap there's a reason. Get recommendations from other companies about who they have used.

Uninsured – Make sure anyone handling your goods is insured if anything goes wrong.

Suppliers won't supply you any more – This can happen if you stock something that's a little old hat or out of date. It may not be economical for your supplier to keep supplying you. Keep your product ranges fresh and up to date. If you've developed a lucrative niche where customers want a rare product make sure you have more than one supplier for those products.

Not listening – If you're having trouble, you've complained several times and nothing's getting done, then move. You're clearly wasting your time with a supplier that doesn't value its customers.

For more information, please visit the website:
www.millionpoundmums.com

or scan the QR code below

CHAPTER TWENTY

AT-A-GLANCE CHECKLIST

Well, it's a lot of information to take in when you decide to start a business. You have to think about the idea, the finance, where you'll work, how you'll get customers, can you do the accounts, have you thought enough about cash flow. And quite apart from thinking about the practical things, you have to take account of your feelings and your family's feelings. How will they feel if you start a business? How will <u>you</u> feel as your project moves from drawing board to drawing room to board room?

> *"Enter a field that you absolutely love because it will provide a buffer against setbacks, hardships and sacrifices you will have to make."*
>
> Lavetta Willis, Co-owner and President, International Shoe Company

Starting a business can feel like a whirlwind with you at the centre. You're trying to think of a thousand things at once, trying to keep all the plates spinning, and all the while trying to be the best mum you can be. It isn't easy, but it's well worth it.

So here's a checklist I've drawn up to help you work through all the things you need to consider as you take this journey. Go through them systematically and tick each one off as you go. It will help you boil down all the information you've gathered into something manageable.

It will also help get you into the habit of planning, and of revising and revisiting your plans as you go along.

So are you ready?

Your personal journey

- Do you understand what starting up a business will really mean to you and your family, how it will affect your individual circumstances? Do you know how you will cope with going it alone, and do you have a strategy for dealing with the difficulties?

- Do your family understand the implications of you starting a business and are they fully on board?

- Have you put in place a system for taking care of your children when you need to work, whether that's hiring childcare or creating a strategy to fit the work around your children?

- Have you worked out what your vision is and how you are going to reach your goal?

- Do you have enough passion for your idea and where will you get your daily inspiration?

- Have you worked out what has made you fearful in the past and have you worked out how to keep any fear in check?

- Do you have a mentor who can guide you?

Have you done the groundwork?

- Have you gathered enough research and have you organised all that data and information so it is useful and usable?

- Have you done your SWOT analysis, thoroughly assessed your strengths and weaknesses, opportunities and threats?

- Have you done your market research? Do you understand the competition and the customers you want? Can you describe what your three main competitors offer and what makes you different? Can you list their strengths and weaknesses, their prices and locations?

- Do you know whether your market is growing, declining or static?

- Have you considered all the necessary factors when pricing: the competition, what your customers are willing to pay, your costs and your profit margin?

- Have you anticipated where the gaps may appear? Have you considered where you will find either staff or outsourcing or the contractors like accountants you will need to run your business? Have you worked out who your partner might be?

- Have you worked out your start up costs and do you know how to raise the finance? Don't forget the small items like a kettle for your kitchen or hidden costs like sudden extra childcare

- Do you know how much money you will need to bring in to survive and pay all your costs? Make sure you have checked for hidden costs like stationery, postage, minimum stock purchase levels, a change in exchange rates or higher bills

- Have you made a decision on whether to register for VAT and do you understand cash flow and book-keeping?

- Have you sourced any grants that are available to you? Have you sourced finance?

- Do you know which tasks you will delegate?

Have you got a plan?

- Have you worked out whether you will be a limited company, a sole trader or a partnership?

- Have you got a business name? Is the name available as a Limited Company? Is the domain name available?

- Do you know what your brand is and have you written down a description of your brand's personality. Do you know what your USP is? Have you worked out your elevator pitch and strapline?

- Have you worked out what the benefits of your products are to customers and what solutions they offer?

- Have you located where your customers go to find information about a product and worked out how you'll communicate with them?

- Do you know how you will generate repeat custom?

- Have you worked out your sales cycle and how long it will take to break even?

- Do you have premises in mind and have you worked out all the costs? Do you have a plan for acquiring it?

- Have you written your business plan?

- Have you written an action plan that is specific, measurable, achievable and relevant with deadlines?

- Have you created a media document with the contact details and web addresses of targeted magazines, newspapers, radio and TV stations and online publications?

- Have you created a marketing plan and do you have the necessary funds or resources to execute it?

- Have you got a social media marketing plan and do you have the time or the staff to keep it going?

- Do you have a plan for growth? What kind of plan is it, are you intending to grow slowly and organically or manically? Can you cope with fast growth if it happens?

- Have you got a strategy for keeping costs down, for instance have you worked out what you could barter or trade or any favours you can ask for?

Have you dotted the Is and crossed the Ts?

- Have you registered your company with the relevant authorities, like Companies House and HMRC?

- Have you registered the domain name?

- Have you protected your business and products with the necessary patents, trademarks or copyright?

- Have you applied for any necessary operating licences or obtained the correct registrations and permission from the relevant statutory bodies? Do you know your health and safety requirements? Have you obtained the necessary certificates for your business?

- Have you got the right business insurances like public liability, car insurance, and employer liability insurance?

- Have you got enough private insurance like private health insurance? There will be no sick pay now so you have to be well, and if you're not you need to get treated quickly and at your convenience. Do you have property insurance? If you are working from home you need to make sure you are covered

- Have you written a customer service policy?

- Have you decided how you will protect your data and your paperwork, especially your client data? How will it be stored? How will you keep back-up information?

- Have you written a contingency plan to cope with emergencies and printed out hard copies?

Are you all geared up?

- Do you have all the necessary computer equipment? Do you have a fast internet connection, a back-up computer, a computer that lets you work on the run like a tablet or a smartphone? Do you have all the necessary software like accounting and cash-flow software? If you are planning to sell online, do you have a website with the right functionality? Do you have the necessary IT backup?

- Have you had a logo designed or come up with ideas for a designer?

- Have you got quotes for business cards, stationery and other materials for your launch?

- Have you found the right business bank for you and have you set up an account? If you have an e-commerce website, have you sourced and set up the best payment system?

- Have you joined relevant business online forums, your industry forums, networks or associations?

- Have you found the right website company who will create a website that functions the way you need it to? Have you asked for references to make sure they can deliver the right design, navigation and back-up?

- Have you got customer database software?

Are you ready to launch?

- Is everything tidy and organised?

- Are you ready to take that leap?

> *"A woman is like a teabag. It's only when she's in hot water that you realise how strong she is."*
>
> Eleanor Roosevelt

For more information, please visit the website:
www.millionpoundmums.com

or scan the QR code below

CHAPTER TWENTY-ONE

STAYING MOTIVATED

Don't skip this chapter because I know you'll be tempted!

You're all fired up with your great idea about the business that's going to make you a million pound mum. And that's great. But there will be days when you wonder why the hell you're doing this. You'll wonder why you didn't stay in a safe job you could leave behind at the end of the day. You'll ask yourself why you should keep going when things are going wrong.

The answer is because it's worth it. But you will need to find ways to remember your motivation and give yourself a break. Things can turn on a sixpence. And just as things can go wrong quickly and you feel like there's a battalion of problems coming towards you, a new customer can turn up and order a shed-load of your products, and suddenly you're flying again. It will be a rollercoaster, but rollercoasters are fun and scary in equal measure.

Be realistic

We have tonnes of plans and we know we can conquer the world, or at least the market we've decided to enter. But there are only so many hours in a day and your partner and children will want a good chunk of them. Start off with what's genuinely manageable even if this means pushing yourself during the time that's available. Three o'clock comes round ever so fast if you have the school run every day, you'll soon be tired, exhausted and running on empty.

You can't run a full-time business on part-time hours so know your limitations and plan accordingly. There's nothing wrong with growing slowly if that's what you can handle. You may need to compromise and put your kids in after-school clubs sometimes, or swap play dates with other working mums – build a network of people you can rely on to help when needed and then it may include emotional as well as practical support.

> *"I will never give up. I never have, even when times have been terrible."*
>
> Michelle Mone, Founder and CEO, Ultimo

Work smart

Be clear about what you need to get done for the big picture on a daily basis. Make sure every task you do feeds into the bigger plan. Don't be a busy fool, prioritise your time. So many business owners waste hours and hours running around being inefficient.

Don't get distracted

Once you have worked out what your daily priorities are, stick to them. It's very tempting to just have a quick look at how many likes you have on Facebook, but checking your social media may not be your task that day. Plan your day and try and stick to it. There will be plenty of days where unexpected things need your attention, so enjoy the days when you can stick to your plan!

Time to knock off

It's very tempting to work around the clock or at least to feel that you should be working. By giving yourself a stop time, you get time with your family and time to relax. Entrepreneurs will tell you that starting a business means working 24/7 and that can be very true. But you can't do that and be a great mum and be productive. Work smart and work less.

Have fun with your kids

It's all too easy to think you don't have time for your children, but they're probably one of the biggest reasons you chose to run your own business in the first place. So make time for them, to take pleasure in their company and have them join in with you and see if they can come up with clever ideas for your business. Ask them if they like having mummy closer to home and not disappearing on a morning commute. Mine loved having me at home and that really kept me going when things were tough.

Julia, Hazel's daughter.

"I learned from watching Mum that you should have courage in your convictions and that you should never do anything half-heartedly. We've seen first-hand that having children doesn't mean you can't run a business. And we've been part of helping Mum's business grow."

Revisit your vision

Day to day it's easy to forget your original vision. Make a

vision board, either a real one or on Pinterest, and remind yourself what you wanted your business to give you. Remember what your end goal is and what you want it to give your life, whether it's financial freedom or the freedom to be your own boss.

I update my vision board regularly – here's a photo of the one I did last year with things I want to achieve in the next five years.

Change your circumstances or routine

Sometimes the smallest change can alter our mood completely. If your four walls are making you stir crazy, go and sit in a café with your laptop for the afternoon. If you've made one particular café your home from home the staff will know you, and you can be instantly lifted by a smile and a chat.

Break it down into chunks

There are some tasks that seem too big to tackle. They hang over your head like the Sword of Damocles and you just can't get the motivation to start them. So just do a bit. Follow the 15 minute rule. Resolve to work on this task for just 15 minutes, you can stand anything for 15 minutes. You will be amazed at the result. By working on it bit by bit, it will get done. Did you ever read your children Aesop's fables, the one about the tortoise and the hare? Well, the tortoise got to the finish line of the race even though he took his time. And you never know, you might actually start the dreaded task, then realise it's not that bad and power through. Sometimes tackling an awful task is a bit like diving into a cold swimming pool, once you're in, it's fine. The hardest part is starting, and knowing that you can stop if you want to makes the task a lot easier. One of the joys of the business growing is that you can start to delegate things you hate – by getting through things you are moving your company forward to that time when it can be someone else's role.

> *"If you are committed to creating value and if you aren't afraid of hard times, obstacles become utterly unimportant. A nuisance perhaps, but with no real power. The world respects creation, people will get out of your way."*
>
> Candice Carpenter, Founder, iVillage.com

Get moving

I find if I sit at my desk all day I get over-stressed or sleepy, especially if it's warm. Get up and walk. Go to the paper shop for a pint of milk. Try and resist the temptation to just walk to the fridge as that's far too easy to do and pretty soon a few extra pounds will have appeared round your waist! Walking energises you and it's great for sharpening your focus and attention. I'm usually at my desk by 7.30am so at 3pm I take half an hour out to walk my dogs – it is a great thinking time for me and I often come back with a solution to a problem or new marketing idea.

Make every day a school day

This is my constant mantra in business, but it's useful for motivation too. It helps you recharge when you read something that sets off a light bulb above your head. You may have been wrestling with a problem then voila! You read something and the answer suddenly appears.

> *"We are only suffering because what we are doing is not big enough for us."*
>
> Debbie Ford, Self Help Author

For more information, please visit the website:
www.millionpoundmums.com

or scan the QR code below

CHAPTER TWENTY-TWO

SELLING UP

It may seem odd to you to talk about selling your business when you are just starting out but it's important to know what you want. Do you want to be running this business for ever or do you need an exit strategy? Are you planning to build it up and sell it so you can either start another business or never have to work again? Start making plans now. As I said at the beginning of this book, you need to know where you're heading if you're going to plan your route properly!

You may not be planning to sell but things can happen that will change your mind. Every business has a lifespan and there are certain signs that perhaps you should think of selling.

What if you get an offer that's too good to turn down? It's very easy to want to hold on to your business, after all it's your baby. But remember why you started the business. If you wanted more freedom and more time with your kids then perhaps the offer is worth considering. If you love running a business you can always start another one, this time with a lovely lump sum in your bank!

Running a business is exciting, but you might find you get bored. Your business won't flourish if you are bored!

You might also find that it's all too much for you because of your age. If you are getting older, why work longer than you have to?

And of course we mustn't forget your family. Your business may be a success but what if your family is suffering? Make sure your partner isn't just being selfish and unsupportive.

But if we assume that you have support but your family life just isn't fulfilling any more, then you need a good think.

Your family will always be more important than your business.

There might also be more technical reasons to sell; you may be forced to consider selling up because of these possible reasons:

You need investment – If you need financing to stay competitive it might make more sense to let someone buy you out. We sold shares in the company to support its growth – this not only helped the cash flow, but bought in a valuable mentor to the business.

Competition – You may have started small, but now the big boys in your field are targeting you. If you can't compete you could go under. They may pay a handsome sum to acquire you or to make you go away.

The market is maturing – If you went into your market as it was growing, it may now have topped out and you've had the best years it's going to give you. You have a choice, you can either adapt, diversify or sell up while there is still some life left in that market.

Making your company attractive to buyers

Even if you can't imagine selling your business, make sure it is attractive to buyers. You may find yourself <u>needing</u> to sell one day, and then it will be difficult to get it in shape in time to find a buyer. Or you may find you have to sell it for far less than you think it's worth, and after all your hard work that would be a huge blow.

There are lots of factors that buyers will use to work out the value of your company. Here are some things you can do to make your company look better to someone who's shopping for a business.

Profits! – It's a no-brainer that a potential buyer will want a profitable company. They want to see that you make money consistently and that if they take over, those profits will stay consistent. They also want to see there's potential for profits to grow.

Staff – If you have done all your homework and put the best team in place then that is an enormous asset. A buyer will need to see that your business can run without you because you have trained and motivated your staff so well.

Intellectual property – You may have a trademark, a patent or copyright on something that is worth a lot. As long as you can prove that property is protected, you might get a buyer.

Repeat customers – If you have managed to create an army of loyal customers that's valuable. As long as your buyer maintains your levels of service then it won't be hard work keeping those customers.

Location – You may find that if you have a premises in a location that's expensive, someone may buy you out because of where you are and not because of what you sell or produce. You may have a really successful cake shop, but if your shop stands in a spot where your buyer could make more money converting the building into a block of flats, then you could make some serious cash.

TOP TIP

A buyer is interested in your bottom line and the potential of your business or your site. They are not interested in your passion or excitement. Try to create something that will be an attractive asset to someone else.

What type of buyer?

So who are your potential buyers? Anyone could be a prospect. A buyer can come from your employees, your customers, suppliers or competitors. People buy businesses for different reasons, and this will affect how you pitch your business to them.

Buyers are usually either strategic or financial buyers. Strategic buyers will look at how well your business fits into their own company's long-range plans. This could be one of your competitors or a large business that wants to enter a new market or offer a new product. If you have what they want, strategic buyers will generally pay you more than other types of buyers. Imagine that you own a second-hand car lot. Someone with a franchise to sell

Toyota cars might want to move into your area. It might make more sense for them to buy you out as you already have planning permission and the right type of site.

Financial buyers are more interested in how profitable and stable your company is. They could either be companies or individuals with money to invest. Some will want a solid, well-managed company that doesn't need too much baby-sitting, while others may specialize in turnaround situations, and they want a business they can tweak to turn a profit.

Finding a buyer

You may end up in the very lucky position of being approached by a buyer. If they come to you that's great. But what if they don't and you want to sell? You don't want to make it too obvious, it's not like selling a car or a house. You don't want to worry your customers by hanging a 'For Sale' sign on the door, they may start to drift elsewhere and then your profits will drop, making you less attractive.

Start with informal chats with people in your network, people like your supplier or your big customers. It might make sense for either of them to take you over if it strengthens their position.

You could also put it to your staff. If you have a keen and motivated team they might be interested in a management buyout.

Talk to your accountant and your business lawyer or your banker. They will have large networks and deal with all kind of businesses. They may make a good matchmaker for you.

If you have grown large enough to worry your competitors then you could approach them directly. If spending money on you gives them more space in the market and more control it may be worth their while.

If you don't strike lucky with these routes you can approach an agent or a broker that specialises in selling businesses.

Getting ready to show

You have to make it easy for any prospective buyer to see your value. Make sure your books are in order showing three years of profit and loss statements, balance sheets, and full tax returns. List all your assets and financial information, and include projections for future earnings.

It's a good idea to create a selling memorandum which starts with an executive summary that tells potential buyers the key elements of your business. You want to provide a list of your products or services and an overview of the industry. They will of course want to know why you are selling so put in an explanation of why you are selling and put a positive spin on it.

What should you expect from the deal?

You have to make some basic decisions when you decide to sell. Are you going to sell the entire business or just the assets? Will you keep any assets? Will the buyer keep your staff? Do you want to retain a minority ownership?

Don't make the mistake of waiting until after the deal is done to remove your assets if they are your personal property. When a buyer walks in he thinks he's buying everything he sees. If you have expensive art on the wall, make sure they know it's not included.

TOP TIP

Don't forget the housekeeping. If they come to view your premises make sure it has good 'kerb appeal' and it's tidy and attractive. If the outside needs painting, paint it. And if your stock room looks like a bombsite, tidy it. It's common sense, but first impressions count. Buyers are only human and if they see you don't care about your premises they'll wonder if you take care of your customers!

How long will it take?

If you've ever sold a house you might know that on average it takes four months to sell. Well it usually takes between 9 months and a year to sell a business. So if you think you might want to sell your business in 18 months' time, then you might want to start the process now and get things in order.

How to walk away

If you've found a buyer that doesn't mean you can just take the cheque and hand them the keys. The new owner may need you for a while, your expertise and knowledge of the customers. Very often buyers will insist you stay on for a period of time to keep everyone loyal and to make sure the hand-over is trouble-free.

The problem is you may not want to do that, you may just want to leave, especially if you want to go for personal reasons. So make sure before you sell that you have created a company that doesn't need you, that can run efficiently with someone else sitting in your chair from day one.

If you are happy to stay on for a while make sure you will get on with your new business partners. You've been used to being number one, so you'll have to adapt.

If you do decide to start another company don't compete with your last one. It isn't good karma, remember the staff are probably people you took on and nurtured. You don't want to put their jobs at risk do you?

And don't dwell on the deal once you have walked. The business was your baby but you have to let it go now. If it suddenly takes off and makes more money don't worry that you shouldn't have sold. You don't know why it took off, it could be because the new owners are killing themselves working 24/7 and never seeing their children. Now you wouldn't want to be that person, would you? Or they may have taken on investors, which means they own less of the business because they've had to give a huge chunk away.

You sold your business, you have the money: enjoy it, enjoy your family, and move on!

For more information, please visit the website:
www.millionpoundmums.com

or scan the QR code below

CHAPTER TWENTY-THREE

THINGS I WISH I'D KNOWN THEN...

... AND WHAT I KNOW NOW!

Very often in business you find that the best bits of advice come out of the experience of other people who've gone before you. Not all of the advice fits into neat little categories, very often it's just a tweak or a casual tip that can give you that 'Aha!' moment. I've made plenty of mistakes and sometimes only got things right because I was forced into a corner. So I hope you can learn something from my experiences. I pass them on to you!

Broke and stuck

It's pretty certain that you will have ideas above your station when you start a business. I certainly did, I knew where I wanted to get to but I didn't have the money to get there. You might find yourself in the same situation. But that shouldn't hold you back, you just have to be innovative and inventive.

When your child calmly announces, usually just as you are putting them to bed, that they forgot to tell you they need a spaceman costume for the morning, you don't say 'Well you can't have one it's too late!' What do you do? You get really creative with the tin foil, gaffer tape and tinsel. Well you can do the same with your business.

When I started Accent Press I managed to get my first book off the ground with very little money. I needed content but couldn't afford to pay for it up front. So I decided to do a charity book and I wrote to famous romantic novelists and asked them for short stories for the book. And they sent them! So my first book was called Sexy Shorts for Christmas and raised money for a breast cancer charity. We got noticed, WH Smith put it in their top 300 stores and we raised money for a really good cause.

> *"Embrace what you don't know, especially in the beginning, because what you don't know can become your greatest asset. It ensures that you will absolutely be doing things different from everybody else."*
>
> Sara Blakely, Founder, Spanx

Soon after starting the company we were offered the chance to go to the Frankfurt Book Fair as part of a Welsh trade delegation. That meant we needed a catalogue of our books. The trouble was, all the publishers there would have glossy catalogues full of their titles but I only had a handful of books! A brochure would have looked really flimsy and exposed the fact that we were a tiny start-up!

Rachel, my assistant at the time, came up with the genius idea of creating a laminated card of each book cover and hooking all of them together on a key chain, then hanging the key chains up on our stall. It was quirky, fun and innovative.

We got all the cards laminated and I got my triplets who were 6 years old at the time to help me assemble them.

They thought it was great fun. So we got to the Frankfurt book fair and everyone wanted to have a look at the key chains because they were different. Being different is the key. We stood out. We took our problem and turned it into a solution. Macmillan distribution, who normally only take on large companies, took us on. We had our first distribution deal, and all because we didn't have enough money or books to do it 'properly'!

I don't know how it's done!

When you're confronted with a task you haven't done before, it's tempting to think you have to know how it's supposed to be done before you do it. Now that may apply to things like book-keeping, or tax and legal obligations, but does it apply to other things? When I was trying to get my first book into shops I had no idea I was 'supposed' to send them the information six months ahead of publication, so I just picked up the phone and rang W.H. Smith. I had no idea that this really wasn't the done thing.

> *"If you obey all the rules you miss all the fun!"*
>
> Katherine Hepburn, Actress

Which is just as well because if I had known, I probably wouldn't have picked up that phone. But it's just as well I did, as I got the book into all their shops almost on the spot!

Think creatively. Sometimes not knowing can actually be a good thing. So never panic!

Let yourself fail

We only ever really learn from mistakes. I once heard someone say that good judgement comes from experience, and experience comes from bad judgement. You are going to make mistakes but don't dwell on them, move on. Don't let any failure make you think that you are a failure. You're not. You're learning to run a business, and that business is like a living organism – it grows and changes and reacts to what's around it. Failures are part of success. Once you embrace that then you have nothing to fear. The only thing that can hold you back is fear of trying again or trying at all.

Make your life easier

Work out whether a small investment will actually make a big difference to your life. You may think you can't afford it, but if it gives you time to work on your business, or the ability to be flexible or spend more time with your family then it might be worth it.

"Be bold. If you're going to make an error, make a doozey, and don't be afraid to hit the ball."

Billie Jean King, Former Tennis Pro

****

"Take successes and failures as they come, since things often change at a moment's notice."

Juliette Brindak, Co-Founder/ CEO, Miss O and Friends

Make every day a school day!

You will know by now that this is the mantra I live by! The more you learn the better equipped you will be to drive your business forward. No information is ever a waste.

Last year I had the opportunity to take part in a 10-month business course run at Swansea University. It was only two days a month but I struggled to take that time out of the business. What I learnt, though, was invaluable, and it also gave me the confidence to write this series of books. I realised that women welcomed the advice and encouragement to start a business but often lacked the confidence to actually do it.

I gained so much from that course and from the other delegates on it – nobody else had a publishing company but we all had very similar issues and concerns about our respective businesses.

My company celebrates its tenth anniversary this year and every single year has been one of growth, change, adapting and learning.

> *"Technology has changed the way we work. Without it, being a working mum would be a very different kettle of fish, and would be much harder. I bought my iPad on the day I started my business, and I have never been without it. It is my most invaluable tool."*
>
> Nicola Sankey, Founder of Choose Nutrition

Tweaks and tricks

Sometimes it's the smallest correction that can get you the biggest result. I guarantee that getting anything right in business is often a process of tweaking rather than huge changes.

For instance, if you sell online and you run out of something, don't put 'Out of Stock' on your website. What message does that send? It tells your customer that you are rubbish at controlling your stock. But what if you put 'Sold Out!' What message would that send to people? It would tell them that the product they want is very popular, so popular it's almost hot, it's flying off the shelves. That will almost certainly make them want it more, it's human nature: if everyone else wants it then we will want it too, it must be good! So you turn your problem into a solution with a simple tweak.

Your children

I started my business because I was stuck in rural Wales with no prospect of a job, 6-year-old triplets and my husband in a foreign country. So there was no time to stop and think if it was a good idea for my children, it had to be! But I made sure that I always had time for my children and I involved them in everything as much as I could so they felt part of what I was doing.

But it turned out better than I could ever have hoped, not just financially but emotionally, for me and my wonderful children. They have grown up in a way I couldn't possibly have imagined. Watching me run my business and helping me with it from such a young age has really had an enormous impact on them. It has helped to teach them the value of work, perseverance, creativity, self-belief and how to never let a failure stop you moving forward.

> *"I've found that you need to move your laptop to a work space. I started downstairs but it was getting in the way of separating mummy time and working time, so now I'm based upstairs. I don't have a laptop in the kitchen or bathroom. Having a distinct area that is for work is the key."*
>
> Caroline Sparks, Founder and Director of Turtle Tots

> *"We set out what's going to be our work time versus our family time, and we'll reassess that... sometimes every week."*
>
> Melinda Gates, Co-Chair, Bill and Melinda Gates Foundation

> *"I have stopped taking my computer with me on holiday. It's a small thing but if you don't have it there's nothing you can do – you have to leave work at home."*
>
> Jessica Anderson, Founder, Jessica's Recipe Bag

I know you might be worried about what effect running your own business will have on your children. But with planning, support and a sense of humour it can work. Support can come from your family, friends, networks you join or the team you surround yourself with. There are always people around who will help when you need it or pick you up when you fall over.

I am so proud of my children and I am so happy I have been able to show them the skills and the values they will need in life by exposing them to the workings of a growing business.

It really is a testament to the benefits of running your own company that all three of my triplets would consider running their own businesses one day. As I write this they're gearing up to apply for university places, but after that who knows? I think it's best if I let them tell you themselves.

Felicity, Julia, and Richard – Hazel's triplets.

Felicity: *"I know I will never have to settle for anything. Mum has showed me that you can achieve what you want by doing something fulfilling. I'd love to start my own business because I've seen Mum do it. When I was 13 I worked up a business plan to see if I could start a business! How many 13 year olds would know how to do that?"*

Julia: *"She's taught me that if you put your mind to it you can do it. She took an idea and made it work. All three of us would consider starting our own businesses."*

Richard*: "We all learned a 'go for it' attitude. What's the worst that can happen? You take calculated risks. Even if it doesn't work out it's a learning curve. You learn to take risks. You learn through the experiences of your parents. It's an important life lesson. We definitely have less fear of failure than other kids."*

Felicity: *"We've learned to be flexible. We're not naive to failure, we're just not afraid of it."*

Julia: *"Mum took me to a trade show when I was 12. It was great fun because we stayed in a hotel and ate burgers from room service and watched X-Factor! But it was great to see what Mum does and I helped her with the selling. She trusted me to help her and it gave me such a huge confidence boost. She showed me she thought I could do it. She always made us feel welcome to help. We have such a strong relationship with her."*

Richard: *"Mum says make every day a school day and we've all taken on that attitude. We love her enthusiasm. She's so optimistic, it's contagious! It's more interesting and exciting and motivating than having a parent who does a 9–5."*

Felicity: *"We know we can do anything but we'll have to work for it. We get to see ALL sides of it, not just the highlights. The Good, the Bad and the Ugly!"*

And finally ...

It is a big undertaking, deciding to start your own business. The highs will be very high and the lows will be pretty deep, too. As I said right at the beginning of this book, this will be the wildest rollercoaster ride of your life. But it will be exciting and it will bring out skills and talents you never knew you had.

You may be just one woman, starting just one business, in just one tiny corner of the world. But it may be the start of something spectacular. Your launch means something. Not just to you but to your whole family. Let that be your guide when you feel overwhelmed or lost. Whatever your business does, it's yours. Yours to build and yours to control.

Tonight, when it's time for bed for your little ones, I am sure your head will be full of ifs and buts and maybes. They'll be swirling in your head as you try and decide if you want to take that leap of faith. But just take a look at your children as you tuck them in. When you go to read them their bedtime story, remember this ...

"You're braver than you believe, stronger than you seem, and smarter than you think."

Christopher Robin, *Pooh's Most Grand Adventure* by A. A. Milne

---

… and this!

> *"Now, get out there and kick ass!"*
>
> Stella McCartney, Fashion Designer

For more information, please visit the website:
www.millionpoundmums.com

or scan the QR code below

How To Be A Million Pound Mum -

25 Great Business Ideas

Hazel Cushion

So you want to be a great mum and, ideally, a rich one too? This range of books offers constructive advice on how to start a business, still be a great mum and have fun while doing it. Together with great advice, this book also contains the experiences and tips of mums who have all successfully started their own companies. Some have reached the Million Pound Mum goal and other are well on the way.

ISBN: 9781908766816 Price £9.99

How To Be A Million Pound Mum -

And Still Have Great Kids

Hazel Cushion

Many mothers dream of starting their own businesses, both for the financial rewards and to give them more flexibility with their family lives and commitments. This book offers clear, easy-to-understand advice on how to achieve this balance so that the whole family can benefit. How should you handle the demands of both your business and children? Which rules will help you achieve a healthy work/ life balance?

ISBN: 9781908766830 Price £9.99

For more information on

Million Pound Mum

scan the QR code below:

Visit www.millionpoundmums.com for up-to-date business advice, tips and hints, and interviews with successful, inspirational people from the world of business.

Accent Press Ltd

Please visit our website
www.accentpress.co.uk
for our latest title information,
to write reviews and
leave feedback.

We'd love to hear from you!